The Last Supper of Chicano Heroes

Camino del Sol

A Latina and Latino Literary Series

The Last Supper
of Chicano Heroes

Selected Works of
JOSÉ ANTONIO BURCIAGA

EDITED BY

Mimi R. Gladstein and Daniel Chacón

The University of Arizona Press *Tucson*

The University of Arizona Press
© 2008 The Arizona Board of Regents
All rights reserved

Library of Congress Cataloging-in-Publication Data

The last supper of Chicano heroes : selected works
of José Antonio Burciaga / edited by Mimi R. Gladstein
and Daniel Chacón.
    p. cm.   (Camino del sol)
  ISBN 978-0-8165-2661-1 (hardcover : alk. paper)—
  ISBN 978-0-8165-2662-8 (pbk. : alk. paper)
   1. Burciaga, José Antonio.   2. Mexican Americans—
Humor.   3. Mexican Americans—Caricatures and
cartoons.   4. Mexican American wit and humor.
5. American wit and humor, Pictorial.   6. Essays.
I. Gladstein, Mimi Reisel.   II. Chacón, Daniel.
PS3552.U66A6   2008
813'.54—dc22   2008005980

Publication of this book is made possible in part by the
proceeds of a permanent endowment created with the assistance of a Challenge Grant from the National Endowment
for the Humanities, a federal agency.

Manufactured in the United States of America on acid-
free, archival-quality paper containing a minimum of 30%
post-consumer waste and processed chlorine free.

13   12   11   10   09   08   6   5   4   3   2   1

for Cecilia Preciado Burciaga

Contents

PART ONE: *Cosas Lingüísticas*

Essays

Poetry

PART TWO: *Cartoons* *63*

PART THREE: *Las Fronteras of Culture Clash*

Essays

Acknowledgments

This project has been a great joy, made more so by the people who have supported us. Cecilia Burciaga provided great encouragement throughout the project, including inviting us into her home and putting up with us for days as we went through box after box of Burciaga's work. Her participation made this book possible. Her generosity was astounding.

Also, thanks to the staff at University of Arizona Press, especially Patti Hartmann, who supported this project from the beginning, and John Mulvihill, our exemplary copyeditor.

We would also like to thank the home team, those at the University of Texas, El Paso, who were behind us from the beginning, including Howard Daudistel, dean of the College of Liberal Arts, and Dennis Bixler-Marquez, director of Chicano Studies. Also, we offer our humble thanks to John Fahey, whose patience at our technological ineptitude made so many things possible.

This book belongs as well to the family and friends of Burciaga, who told us so many wonderful anecdotes about the man, memories that constantly reinforced the importance of this collection.

DANIEL CHACÓN *and* MIMI R. GLADSTEIN

The Last Supper of Chicano Heroes

Editors' Introduction

Although it can be argued that the roots of Chicano/a literature began with the conquest itself, we can look at the Chicano/a Movement of the 1960s and 1970s as the source of its formal elements, most of which derived from protest against racism, lack of representation in public institutions, and the Vietnam War. Much of the literature itself was conceived as a form of protest. In fact, in the beginning of the Chicano/a literary movement, the political and the social messages were more important than issues of art and craft. *Rasquache* refers not only to the mixture of "lowbrow" and "highbrow" art (everyday images surrounding the Chicano/a home have been used as aesthetic subjects), but to the oftentimes crude manner in which the art was put together. If the purpose of Chicano/a visual art (poster art) was to quickly mobilize the people, then an artist would create an image with whatever available material he or she had. "Actos," the short plays written and performed by El Teatro Campesino, were performed on the back of flatbed trucks or on the street. The important thing was to get the message out: Boycott grapes. Boycott Coors. ¡Huelga!

Similarly, with Chicano/a literature what was more important than careful multiple revisions and conventional formal considerations was distribution of the message itself. The purpose was to mobilize, educate, and empower. A survey of early Chicano/a literary journals demonstrates that grammatical considerations were often subordinated to the social-political message.

The elements of Chicano/a verbal and visual art that made up the initial de facto forms came from the immediate situation, which was a call to protest and rebellion. Therefore, if we ask of the early Chicano/a artists, For whom did they create? the answer would inevitably be: "for *la gente*." The conscious elements of Chicano/a art and literature are rebellion, identity (cultural affirmation), and empowerment (call to action). Chicano/a literature did not desire to have its place among mainstream literature until later. It must be remembered that these initial characteristics gave way, as the Movement matured and grew, to wider distribution and attention to craft as well as an awareness of its own form. However, it is still true, as of this writing in the year 2006, that literature that identifies itself as "Chicano/a," to some extent, contains the same elements: rebellion, identity, and empowerment. The difference between Chicano/a literature and "literature which happens to be written by a Chicano/a" (or a Hispanic) is exactly that: one consciously or unconsciously identifies with the values of the Movement, which is to say political social activism; the other does not.

José Antonio "Tony" Burciaga was among the first Chicano/a writers and artists whose work forms a passage (*el paso*) between the initial elements of Chicano/a literature and the Chicano/a literature of today, which may subordinate social issues. Burciaga not only offered art to *la gente* through his literature and images, but he cared about art itself. His work is definitely accessible to almost anyone.

Not only is Burciaga important because his work forms a bridge between the early Chicano/a artists and those of today, but he is a multidisciplinary artist, equally adept at creating artistic truth through the medium of words or the medium of images. For this reason he may fall through the cracks of criticism, which tends to be discipline specific. Because of his amazing versatility, he often defied categorization. He worked in a variety of genres. Burciaga was a poet, a journalist, an essayist, and a short story writer. Some have called him a humorist. His cartoons, murals, and drawings are seminal images of the early years of the Chicano/a Movement.

Burciaga published books, newspaper articles, and cartoons and produced major Movement images. His earliest book publication was the self-published *Restless Serpents* (1976), an out of the ordinary poetry collaboration that had two front covers. One was the cover for seventy-four pages of poems by Bernice Zamora; the other introduced a sixty-four-page poetry collection by Burciaga. This project itself reflects both the spirit of community and the character of Burciaga, because it is a communal project, a public expression that includes the male and the female voice.

Burciaga was also a talented comic performer, one of the founding members of the comedy troupe Culture Clash (1984). He wrote and performed short skits and monologues addressing the social-political issues of the Movement and the Chicano/a experience, a sort of passive resistance. This group was cutting edge in the sense that it not only critiqued the standard activist issues, but in postmodern fashion, it also made fun of the Movement itself, sometime harsh self-criticism about ideology and commitment.

In 1988 his first major essay anthology *Weedee Peepo* was published. It was followed by *Drink Cultura* (1992) and *Spilling the Beans* (1995). Some of the pieces in these anthologies had been published earlier in journals or newspapers. *Undocumented Love* (1992) is an anthology of poetry that also contains numerous drawings, including the famous Drink Cultura image that appears on the cover of the book of the same name. The book was honored with a Before Columbus prize from the American Book Awards. In 1995 Burciaga was presented with the National Hispanic Heritage Award.

Burciaga did not move away from his primary interest in the social and cultural reality of Chicanos/as; he would, rather, become more developed and knowledgeable in the study. If he wasn't writing, painting, or spending time with his family or in the community, he was reading books in Spanish and English, studying literature, politics, history, and cultural values and their linguistic expressions. He was fascinated with folk wit and linguistic traditions. In *In Few Words/En pocas palabras*, he collected *dichos*, popular sayings among Mexicans and other proverbs in the Spanish language. This book was published in 1997 and is still in print. We include some of his favorite dichos to introduce many chapters, such as, "Hay quien mucho cacarea y nunca pone un huevo!"—A lot of people cackle, but never lay an egg.

Burciaga produced a lot of good work in his short life, *para la gente*, and now, in this collection, we present his gift to those he left behind. The majority of this work deals with social-cultural issues, language, and food.

An often painful source of alienation for the Chicano/a people in the 1960s, 1970s, and beyond is the dominant culture's misunderstandings based on language and other cultural differences. Many Chicano/a children have learned early in their lives to deny their own culture, to deny their own Chicanismo. As recently as a generation ago in El Paso, Texas, students who spoke Spanish in public schools were punished and subject to what was called Spanish detention. It was simply not allowed to speak Spanish in schools, even when the majority in some schools were Spanish speakers. They were made to feel ashamed of the food they ate, the language they spoke, the way they dressed, the appearance of their family members, and many everyday details in the life of Chicanos/as. Cultural affirmation on the part of Chicano/a artists refers not only to refusing the demand to hide your Chicanismo, but also in celebrating your culture. Institutions within the dominant culture have made Chicanos/as feel ashamed for speaking Spanish. Traditional Mexicans have made them feel ashamed for not speaking Spanish very well. Chicano/a artists and writers, however, recognize that the language spoken by Chicanos/as—a mixture of Spanish and English with a lot of Chicanismo sprinkled in—is linguistically beautiful and rich.

Burciaga not only addresses these issues within his work, but he makes it understandable and funny. Chicano/a schoolchildren all over the United States have experienced the embarrassment and the alienation of their lunch in the schoolyard. In the poem "Skool Daze," Burciaga writes,

> Un burrito de chorizo con huevos
> stained my brown paper bag y los kakis
> while Suzy looked on,
> her Roy Rogers lunchbox
> hanging and laughing
> with peanut butter jelly sandwiches.

Not only do we have the mixture of languages, called code switching, but also the mixture of cultures. This Chicano child feels that he does not measure up simply based on what lunch he brings to school. In this poem, the speaker has a brown paper bag stained with grease, because inside is a burrito. By contrast, little Suzy is clearly connected through her possession of a Roy Rogers lunchbox to the dominant culture. Hidden within the subtext is the fact that Suzy's family can provide her with a lunchbox, whereas the Chicano/a student must take his lunch in an everyday brown paper bag. In fact, why is Suzy's lunchbox "hanging and laughing"? It is as if the object itself is aware of or assumes its own superiority over the grease-stained, brown paper bag. But it's not just the exterior person—the khakis and the brown paper bag—that is subject to judgment, but also what is inside. What can be more American than peanut butter and jelly on white bread? What can be more un-American than "un burrito de chorizo con huevos"? A burrito is made with a tortilla, the Chicano/a bread of life. It is perhaps important to note that the flour tortilla with which burritos are made is not a common food item in Mexico. In Mexico the tortilla is made of corn, but in Chicanolandía the flour tortilla is more common.

Suzy's perspective would have the Chicano/a be ashamed of who he is. Chorizo is Mexican sausage, a basic item of the Mexican diet. Roy Rogers, all-American, laughs at the Chicano/a. The American girl laughs at the grease-stained paper bag.

Later in the poem, Burciaga writes,

Memo got pissed
porque la ticha had told him,
"Tuck your shirt in!"
and so he tucked in his guayabera.

For Chicanos/as this particular passage is humorous as well as affirming. La ticha refers to the way a Chicano/a child would pronounce the teacher. The teacher is clearly not a Latina, because any Mexican knows that you do not tuck in a guayabera. It is a formal dress shirt that is worn as a combination shirt and jacket. That the teacher would apply her standards to that particular garment shows that she is not aware of the cultural significance of such a shirt. This passage refers to those cultural misunderstandings, those "cultural clashes," that are an integral part of the Chicano/a experience and of which Burciaga writes so well.

There is also something affirming for the Chicano/a in this particular passage in that only those initiated into the culture will understand the humor. It is like an inside joke, and in that way it is empowering. We may be ostracized by our cultural differences, but we are also unified by those same differences. "La gente unida jamás sera vencida."

Burciaga was an activist. Activism is a thankless job. The fruits of the labor do not come until after the political event in which the activist has invested his or herself, and often those who benefit are not even aware of who fought for them. The beneficiaries were not even present when the protest posters were made, when the all-night vigils were held; they do not know about the jail cells where activists were incarcerated, sometimes after being maced by riot police. They do not know of the legal battles with universities that led to many activists losing their jobs. It has never been easy to be a Chicano/a activist, and at times the activists incur the disdain of the very people they are trying to protect. People from the community may tell them not to make waves, or they do not understand why they have to draw so much attention to themselves. In a sense, activism, whether it's for the Chicano/a Movement, the black movement, the women's movement, or any other movement, is led by selfless leaders, or at the very least, those who have accepted that personal sacrifice may be involved.

Burciaga has done more for the Chicano/a people than many in his or subsequent generations realize. One of the most culturally affirming images in Chicano/a iconography is the Drink Cultura image that Burciaga created in parody of popular culture and to assert Chicano/a culture. He takes the colors of the Coca-Cola label and changes them to the colors of the Mexican flag. And he offers a familiar drink, *cultura*, culture, not the manufactured liquid of a large corporation, but the *sabor* of a unique way of life, of things that are Chicano/a. This image is more famous than the artist himself. You often see young people wearing T-shirts of that image, or you'll see it on bumper stickers. A famous expression among Chicanos/as comes from Burciaga and is perhaps another creation more famous than the creator: "We didn't cross the border, the border crossed us."

But perhaps the most famous Chicano/a image (and we mean in all of Chicano/a art) is *The Last Supper of Chicano Heroes*, which Burciaga designed and painted on the walls of the Casa Zapata at Stanford University. It is the Chicano/a version of Da Vinci's *Last Supper*. Burciaga's essay of the same name (included in this collection) addresses this subject. There were so many activists that enhanced the lives of the Chicano/a people that it was impossible for Burciaga to choose only twelve, and why invite only twelve people to a *pachanga*, a big party? This was, after all, the Chicano/a version, and everybody is welcome. Burciaga invited so many people to the banquet that not all of them could fit at the table, and instead of putting the Chicano/a apostles in the interior of an inn, he put them in a cornfield. Even the sacred cornstalks that stretch all the way to the horizon have the shapes and the spirit of the people, those who have toiled in the fields and have fought for the rights that we take for granted today. Sitting at the table are the most recognizable Chicano icons, including Emiliano Zapata, Cesar Chavez, Benito Juárez, and Gregorio Cortez. But he also placed there sor Juana Inés de la Cruz, the Mexican nun, who was a brilliant poet and essayist, and could perhaps be considered the first Chicana feminist. He also included Frida Kahlo, another very important symbol to the Chicana experience. To have placed only men at the table would not have reflected the true spirit of the Chicano/a Movement, but rather the early undeveloped aspects of its sexism. He also included Martin Luther King Jr., who, although not a Chicano/a, helped define the nonviolent elements with which the Chicano/a Movement would ultimately identify itself and would feed into the ideology of Cesar Chavez and the United Farm Workers movement.

But who could be the Chicano/a Christ? You can imagine the controversy that this mural could have caused among the Chicano/a people had Burciaga chosen the wrong Christ-like figure for this image. His choice was brilliant. He chose not a Chicano/a, but an icon to the Chicano/a Movement, one of the most recognized icons among people everywhere: Che Guevara, who, like the image of Christ, can mean many things to many people. For those who consider themselves defenders of, or members of an oppressed people, Che's example is perfect. He took up arms for the revolution, giving up a promising medical career and the comforts of upper-class living.

He was perhaps the only image that could have been placed as the Christ-like figure at the head of this Chicano/a table without causing arguments. It's also important to note that in *The Last Supper of Chicano Heroes*, standing behind Che's chair, is a skeleton, an image that evokes the work of Mexican artist José Guadalupe Posadas, whose drawings and paintings of *calaveras* are the models for the skeletons we see today all over Mexico during the Day of the Dead, skeletons having a party, skeletons sitting at a table raising glasses, the dead doing the everyday activities of the living. With the inclusion of this skeleton, Burciaga is identifying Chicano/a art with the Mexican tradition. This also identifies the Chicano/a relationship with the dead. It's not just those whose songs have been sung that have brought us to where we are today, but it is the common dead, and we do not forget them. A little known fact about this famous image is that in the right-hand corner are two people, a man and a woman, whom most people will not recognize. They are the artist's mother and father, Cruz and María Burciaga. By including them among the heroes, Burciaga not only honors his own family and roots, those who gave him life, but also the *idea* of family, the respect for parents, for elders, for *antepasados*. In other works, Burciaga expresses his opinion on how Mexicans see the dead as existing side by side with the living. In the United States people often avoid the word "death," preferring euphemisms such as "passed away" or is "not with us anymore."

Also important to note are the presence of popular culture figures like Carlos Santana. This is an affirmation that we are not only activists but also musicians. Part of the Chicano/a soul is expressed through the music. Santana not only played rock 'n' roll, but he did it with a Latino beat, bongos and all.

The entire image is framed on both sides by indigenous religious icons of pre-Columbian Mexico. Above everybody—floating in the air—is la Virgen de Guadalupe, who is indigenous. She spoke the Aztec language of Nahuatl when she appeared to Juan Diego, and she has indigenous features and brown skin, la Morenita, the little brown one. She is the mother of the oppressed. She is the most important religious figure in the Mexican-Chicano/a experience. Her image was used to defeat the Spaniards when the Mexicans fought for independence from Spain. Her image was used in California to lead the farmworkers on strike. She is the mother of the downtrodden. In many Mexican households she is as important as the son she bore. In fact, presented for the first time in this collection is an array of images of la Virgen de Guadalupe. We call it the "Virgin Variations," and it is very clear that each image has a particular energy that is specific to the Chicano/a experience. It is also clear that Burciaga not only understands her importance, but senses her divinity. She means so many things, all of them positive, all of them affirming, all of them with their roots in the indigenous experience, that to try to understand the Chicano/a Movement without including her would be a grave mistake. That is why she has the divine presence in this image, *The Last Supper of Chicano Heroes*. She is the Holy Mother. She is the goddess of the Americas.

The *Last Supper of Chicano Heroes* image that Burciaga painted on the wall at Stanford University is not a rejection of the European model; rather it is to show how Chicanos/as can fit into and understand their history and religious beliefs within the structure of the dominant culture. Burciaga was revolutionary, but he did not concern himself with plotting the overthrow of the U.S. government. He was not a strict party-liner. Like most Chicano/a activists of his generation, he embraced revolutionary imagery, but he voted, not out of deep loyalty to a political party, but as the most practical means of addressing the issues that concerned him, including poverty, and he served for many years in the U.S. Air Force.

Underneath this painting, Burciaga included the words "and to all those who died, scrubbed floors, wept and fought for us." Why does it say "scrubbed floors"? Clearly the people who have worked scrubbing floors as maids, picking fruit in the fields, paying the bills, and feeding their families are just as important as every single famous person in that image. This is Chicanismo. This is Chicano/a expression.

It remains today one of the most popular images in all Chicano/a art, and certainly among the most recognizable. But how many people, upon seeing it, know that Burciaga was the artist? Not many. But activism is a thankless job.

On a lighter note, the section on "Cooks and Comidas" demonstrates Burciaga's early understanding of the role of food both as a repository and ambassador of the culture. Long before reference works and scholarly journals incorporated articles on the connections between food and literature as well as between food and culture, Burciaga routinely included essays about food and its role in the community as part of his anthologies. Meredith Abarca, writing in the *Oxford Encyclopedia of Latinos and Latinas in the*

United States, uses a culinary metaphor to describe how Latina and Latino literature uses food to convey some of the paradoxes and issues of life. They often offer "a *salpicón*," some of this and that, "as the best recipes are created." The "Cooks and Comidas" section follows just that recipe. In one cartoon, appropriately titled, "Los Changing Times . . . ," a man orders a kosher New York pastrami burrito. In another, a Martian's first query is not "Take me to your leader," but "Where can you get good Mexican food?" Burciaga's sense of the absurd was tickled by things like Mexican pizza, and he pushed the envelope on such possibilities. In his comic sketches for Culture Clash, he would pull out a *molinillo*, a wooden implement used to stir up hot chocolate, then attach an electric cord to it and claim it to be a Chicano Mix Master, the subtextual message being that what Chicanos/as possess is of no less value than what the consumer culture defines as important to the process. He might say, "¡Migajas también son pan y buen alimento dan!"—Crumbs are bread too, and will also nourish you.

It is important to note that in all of Burciaga's work, he never exhibits sexism, even in culinary matters of the kitchen, the "traditional" place for Chicana women. The essays appeal to both genders. Burciaga does not buy into the sexism or machismo that plagued the early civil rights movements. In fact, when he was creating the book of dichos, *En pocas palabras*, he made the choice to eliminate those that involved negative or sexist views of women. He would not have that kind of energy in his work.

There were and still are, in some segments of the various rights movements, internal problems of discrimination. In the sixties and seventies, although both men and women were marching, being jailed, and suffering the results of oppression, when the groups went into strategy or policy-making sessions, women were told to "Go make the coffee." In Burciaga's works there is a decided lack of any "macho" pose or tone. When he shares his family recipes, there is no gender differentiation as to who is supposed to be doing the cooking.

The demonstration of his humorous tone begins with the titles, where he employs puns and double entendre, as well as allusion. For example, "I Remember Masa" is clearly an allusion to the film and book *I Remember Mama*. Both were popular in his youth. In "Flour Power," he is making a pun on the slogan of the hippies, the flower children, who would put flowers into the gun barrels of troops deployed to control them.

In "Consuming Passions," Burciaga plays on the double meaning of the word "consuming," which can mean, in separate contexts, eating or being eaten. The family recipes he shares are to be consumed, but his appreciation for tortillas and things made from tortillas has consumed him throughout his life. The essay displays his multicultural perspective when he refers to *albóndigas* as "Mexican meat matzo balls." Another metaphor for Burciaga's essays is that they operate a bit like *apertivos*; that is, they are not a full meal, but enough to stir the appetite or inspire conversation and variations on the themes he introduces.

In the essays in "Cosas Lingüísticas," Burciaga has a lot of fun thinking about language. He points out the humor of mispronunciation and misunderstanding on the part of monolingual English speakers of Spanish words, as well as native Spanish speakers mispronouncing and misunderstanding English words. For example, if a Chicano/a child calls a teacher a *culero*, he's basically saying that the teacher is an asshole. But teachers who do not know Spanish may be proud that their "Hispanic" students are calling them a "cool arrow." A Chicano/a kid might watch a scary movie on TV, starring their favorite horror movie actor, Mr. Beans and Rice, Vincent Price. Burciaga's brother tells how when the kids grew up underneath a Jewish synagogue in El Paso, they didn't understand why every Saturday their father would greet the congregants by saying "Good Chavez" (Good Shabbos).

But with linguistic considerations, the truth is not just humorous. One of the serious issues about bilingualism is the threat others feel when some of the population can function in two languages. There have been many pushes in California and other southwestern states to require English only, in a sense to get rid of bilingualism. Although this issue is of deep concern for Burciaga, as it was for much of the Chicano/a community, he was able to find humor in the situation. He took what he perceived as a racist position (the elimination of bilingualism) to its illogical conclusion. Would Boca Raton, Florida, be such a desirable address if it were referred to in English? Who would want to live in Rat's Mouth? And who in their right mind would ever want to live in Bathrooms, California (Los Banos)? This joke (the ridiculousness) of changing Spanish names of towns in California and throughout the United States has become a staple in Chicano/a comedy, a cultural counterpart, if you will, to the knock-knock joke, but Burciaga was certainly its innovator. It was Burciaga who told us that nobody would want to visit relatives in Lard, California (Manteca). In fact, this is the case with a lot of Burciaga's linguistic and imagistic innovations. They have so seeped into everyday Chicano/a culture, that we use his idioms and images and articulate his ideas without realizing the source.

Burciaga recognizes an analogy between the Chicano/a who was often called an illegal alien and the world's most famous alien, the one from outer space, E.T. He tells us that he cannot relate to the family that found

E.T., because that kind of upper-middle-class lifestyle was unknown to him; but he "did relate to E.T., the funny little creature from outer space." Burciaga explained: "All of us use nontraditional modes of transportation to get here. E.T. had his spaceship. I know of other illegal aliens who arrived in the trunks of automobiles, on water wings, in railroad refrigerator cars, or were catapulted over the fence by friends using a teeter-totter-like contraption."

He speaks also of the way the alien is received into the dominant culture. First there is curiosity, followed by fear. "My earliest encounter was at a swimming pool not normally frequented by Mexican-American kids. Three blonde boys studied me from a distance before finally coming over to ask me if I was a pachuco" (an urban Chicano identified by his style of dress). "I said no, but they didn't believe me. They ran away yelling, 'A pachuco! A pachuco!'"

The final section of this anthology is made up of excerpts from *The Temple Gang*, the book that Burciaga was in the process of writing when he died. In the *San Jose Mercury News* on July 24 of 1995, just a few years before Burciaga's death at the age of fifty-seven, Jeordan Legon tells of Burciaga's struggle to write his last works. Burciaga explained his frustration with the weakness created by a series of operations and radiation and numerous trips to the doctors: "You have to be well enough spiritually and emotionally to put yourself down on paper and express yourself and have fun with it." Perhaps *The Temple Gang* would have been his magnum opus, because it is clearly very close to his heart, his experience, and the loves of his life: family, El Paso, and the community, including the Jewish synagogue under which his Catholic family lived.

As he prepared to write his memoir, what he calls a "familiography" since it was about more than his own story of the unique experience of going to Catholic schools while living in a Jewish synagogue, Burciaga queried many of his old friends from El Paso to make sure that his memories were accurate. He wanted to corroborate his remembrances of the various rabbis who served the synagogue while his family lived there. More than the story of himself, he was interested in focusing on the story of his father and the congregation. His communications of the time are poignant, as he tried, like the poet John Keats dying two centuries earlier of consumption, to get as much written as possible before the end.

Riffing on the theme song from *The Beverly Hillbillies*, a popular TV show of the times, Burciaga writes: "This here story is about a man named Cruz." However, the chapter soon moves to more serious matters, such as discrimination against immigrants in the United States, emigrants in Mexico, and the anti-Semitism of the Catholic church. The chapter on "Rabbi Joseph M. Roth" is mainly a serious mini-lesson on Judaism, but Burciaga's keen sense of the little inherent ironies of life for his family situation peeks through. He muses about how the framed "Our Lady of Guadalupe, so used to 'Las Mañanitas' by mariachis, would now be greeted by the Jewish shofar."

In reading these excerpts from the unfinished volume, it is important to remember that they are not a final product. They are the thoughts Burciaga was trying to get down as quickly as possible while he was battling his cancer. Still, his sense of humor and a warm nostalgia shine through. The chapter on Jake Ehrlich, who was a member of the congregation and the tallest man in the world at that time, is both a tribute to this gentle giant and a charming reconstruction of his effect on the children who were sure he must be God coming to the temple to pick up his tithe monies.

Generally, Burciaga is the most modest of men, self-effacing and even prone to make fun of himself to make a point. That is why the chapter on "Work and Football" is noteworthy. Not only does it serve as a lesson on the benefits of perseverance, but it is one of the rare occasions when Burciaga presents himself as the hero of his own story. Though short and small, he worked hard and finally made the All City Junior Varsity team. He calls it his most meaningful personal victory.

He has a witty take on the near-sacrifice of Isaac, a charming tale of how Burciaga took a Jewish calendar illustration of the story to his Sister Mary Lambert's class at St. Patrick's.

For the most part, the excerpts included are of nostalgic or humorous bent. However, the fullness of José Antonio Burciaga's complex personality would not be adequately represented without the inclusion of his chapter "Mexico, Loved and Surreal." In "¡Adelante!" our story of compiling this volume, we touch upon Burciaga's sense of the metaphysical, the ever-present reality of death. As he puts it, "Mexico is closer to an ancient culture and the reality of death." How fitting it was that the University of California at Santa Barbara chose to honor José Antonio Burciaga with an exhibition altar and readings on the Day of the Dead. In this chapter, Burciaga recounts a spiritual experience, seeing his dead father on a pyramid in Mexico.

José Antonio Burciaga died on October 7 of 1996 after a long battle with cancer. In his shortened span of years, he accomplished a great deal. The following year House Resolution 1310 was put before the Texas legislature calling on the 75th Texas legislature to pay tribute to Burciaga's memory by honoring him posthumously as a "Texas Treasure in light of his exceptional contributions to the history and culture of the Lone Star State."

But of course his influence is not limited to Texas. Burciaga has been translated into many languages and is studied all over the world. The editorial cartoons he penned under the name of El Indio Hispanic have been cut out and hung on bulletin boards, walls, and doors all over the country, with few people even realizing who was the artist. His brand of humor has not only influenced countless Chicano/a artists and writers and performers, but has provided slogans for entire political social movements. With the proliferation and maturation of Chicano/a literature, a certain level of sophistication is inevitable. Among the young, the word Chicano/a is often spelled Xican@, the end symbol being nongendered, neither male nor female, but the voice of a community, which is both. With this new level of sophistication, this new generation of writers and artists and activists, many of the veterans of the early Chicano literary movement have fallen by the wayside, because their work as we see it now is sexist or poorly constructed or at any rate unsophisticated in its technique and form. In fact, a lot of this Chicano literature, if it is studied today, may be studied more for its historical significance than its artistic merit, much the same way we may still value Upton Sinclair's *The Jungle*. This novel may be used in history and sociology courses, but its didactic tone often keeps it out of classes whose emphasis is Great Books. Similarly, much of the early Chicano/a literature is no longer studied in Chicano/a literature courses. The classics of Chicano/a literature, those that will remain through time great works of art, are classics because they are consistent with the values of the movement and are well constructed. The Xican@ Movement continues to grow in its ideological and artistic sophistication. Writers like Sandra Cisneros not only cross over to larger audiences and become best-sellers, studied in English departments and graduate seminars, but the work stays true to the values of the Xican@ Movement, especially the issues of class and gender. Xican@ literature has little patience with sexism; so many of the early writers may not be studied because of the male-dominated, sexist perspective. José Antonio Burciaga will always be studied, not only because his values are consistent with the Chicano/a Movement and the Xican@ Movement (a glaring lack of macho perspective) but also because of the formal and technical innovation. We can still learn from him. We do still learn from him. He still feeds us. This "salpicón" of a volume is the best of his work, a delicious caldo de pollo for the Xican@ soul.

REFLECTION

Reflection. In this image, somewhat postmodern in its comment on the act of creation, the artist creates (consciously or unconsciously) reflections of the self. This captures Burciaga in one of his more playful moods.

¡Adelante!

Death is contagious.
—JOSÉ ANTONIO BURCIAGA

*T*he dead man sat on a chair and pointed to the forty-one white card-board boxes. All of them contained a lifetime of letters, art, and essays, posthumous things that had to do with his life as an artist, a political pundit, and a Chicano writer ¡con safos y que! These forty-one white boxes, neatly arranged in a square in the middle of a light blue carpet, were in the Carmel home basement. They almost looked like a flotilla of white boats on the sea, on the shore of which we stood, Daniel Chacón, Chicano writer, and Mimi Gladstein, literature professor. Cecilia Burciaga, the dead man's wife, stood at the top of the stairs. "There they are," she said, looking sadly at the boxes, at the empty chair where the dead man sat. "All of them. Use whatever you want."

Chacón looked at his watch, wondering if they would have enough time. He looked at Gladstein, who was looking at the perfect row of boxes. She wondered why it had taken her so long to accept the invitation. Tony had invited her often; how much better it would have been if he had been at the door to meet her with their customary abrazo.

The chair in that basement looked empty, and it was the only furniture in the room. Most of our work there was done sitting on the floor. When we had first descended into the basement all that had been on the wooden chair—which Cecilia had gotten from her work at Stanford—was a book. Other than the forty-one boxes of Tony's "stuff," the chair and the book were the only things in the room. The book was called *Ghost Story Encyclopedia*. Chacón picked it up and saw that it was an alphabetical dictionary of ghost stories and imagery.

When asked about the book, Cecilia said that it didn't belong to Tony, but to her son, and she did not know why it was in the basement with his stuff or how it even got down there. Tony chuckled.

Were Tony, that is, José Antonio Burciaga, alive today, were he reading this introduction to his best and posthumous work, edited by Chacón and Gladstein, he would have no trouble believing that the dead can walk side by side with the living. He wouldn't have to "suspend disbelief," because he did not see the world in a purely material way, in a way that he might have jokingly referred to as the gringo way of seeing. One of his essays proposed that as *Life* had been such a popular magazine, there should also be a magazine called *Death*, everything you would need to know about living with the dead, and everything you would want to read about being dead, including a recipe section with directions for making *pan de muerto* and candy skulls, for Mexico's Day of the Dead. He knew there were other worlds, other perspectives, other realities, and this could be seen in his opinion articles, whose political positions were not of the mainstream Democrat or Republican but from the Chicano perspective. It is no accident that today Burciaga is among the most respected veteranos among Chicanos. He weaved his way through life seeking love and kindness, not profit and personal advancement. He was able to experience, like many Mexicanos and Chicanos, separate realities. He believed in what our ancestors taught him.

Once, when he was still alive, he was sitting in the back of a VW taxi driving through Mexico City, on his way to spend an afternoon in Coyoacán—the barrio where Frida Kahlo lived in a bright purple house. He passed a pyramid—ancient stones put in place by his ancestors—and saw his father, years dead, sitting atop a rock. Tony pressed his hands to the window and got a closer look. It was definitely his dead father sitting on that pyramid, not metaphorically, not thematically or emotionally (although that too), but *actually*. Tony was not surprised that he would see a dead man as real as anyone else on the "surreal" streets of Mexico City. "All my relatives, dead and alive, are scattered throughout Mexico," he wrote. "While in the United States the culture feigns youth and life."

We spent a weekend in that basement with the forty-one boxes—going through works never before seen or not seen in years, reading original copies of his most famous essays, which appeared in the published books *Weedee Peepo*, *Drink Cultura*, *Spilling the Beans*, and *Undocumented Love*. We read each other tidbits from *In Few Words/En pocas palabras*, his compendium of Latino folk wit and wisdom. This anthology includes samples from all the above, but there is also much more. We marveled at the sketches he had drawn of his friends at parties or in cafés on cocktail napkins or whatever paper was available, some of which we include here. A few boxes were full of sketch pads he had filled throughout his life, drawings never before seen by the public, published here for the first time. In one sketch pad he had drawn various images of la Virgencita, and there was one folder of political cartoons that had appeared years earlier in the op-ed section of U.S. newspapers, signed "El Indio Hispanic," one of Tony's pseudonyms. They speak to the wide and varied talents of the man and therefore belong in this anthology.

We read letters and essays and as yet unpublished short stories, and we reveled over his work in progress, an unfinished memoir called *The Temple Gang*. We have chosen what we hope is a sample of the best and most important work of a great artist, writer, humorist, and man.

The form of this book grew out of our experience compiling it; somehow we knew as we sorted through the boxes what the classifications of the parts would be. Tony loved to write of culture, and one of the ways by which he understood and taught us was through food. And so, naturally, among the sections we have one titled "Las Fronteras of Culture Clash" and another "Cooks and Comidas." In "A Mixed Tex-Cal Marriage" (published in *Drink Cultura* but not included in the present collection) Tony writes of the culinary wars between him and his wife, Cecilia. He was a native of El Paso, she of California, and that led to some serious *pleitos* about the right way to eat and cook *comida mexicana* and who has the *mejor* tortilla. He wrote of salsa and bread and tamales (and he reminded us that one tamal is not a tamale but a *tamal*). Tony's multicultural upbringing is highlighted in "An Anglo, Jewish, Mexican Christmas."

It tickled us to think what essay he might write about the low-carb tortilla—what metaphor he would devise for this meshing of U.S. diet culture and the Mexican-American experience. He probably would have found it ironic, yet he would be able to make sense of it. In "The Great Taco War," he writes about a Taco Bell opening its doors in Mexico City and asks how it was that the capital of Mexican culture and food would import a gringo representation of Mexican food. Perhaps, he surmised, the restaurant is for North American tourists, who, overwhelmed by too much Mexico in Mexico, need to return to the comfort food of home, back to the Enchorito and the Mexican Pizza.

Like most good writers, he was fascinated with the peculiarities of language. The "Cosas Lingüísticas" section contains several of his musings on the subject. Here we have included the comic, such as "Pendejismo," and some that, with their dollop of humor, approach more serious topics, as in "What's in a Spanish Name?"

A Burciaga reader, however, should represent the man in all his artistic accomplishment. Tony Burciaga distinguished himself from most artists in his versatility, in his command of many artistic media. He was both a verbal and a visual artist; he was adept as cartoonist, portraitist, and muralist. As mentioned earlier, we marveled at the drawings we had never seen, but we also felt compelled to include the famous works, such as "The Last Supper of Chicano Heroes." Only by including both the celebrated and the undiscovered artwork is this anthology properly suggestive of Burciaga's considerable talents.

In addition to the previously published works included in the sections on language, culture, and food, we have included previously unpublished works, including *The Temple Gang*, the memoir that Tony was working on in his last years. We believe that this anthology, put together with the help of Tony and Cecilia, is important, not only for the Chicano literary canon, but also for the preservation of a culture itself, the Chicano creative, spiritual, and political voice. We cannot separate Tony from his politics any more than we can separate him from his Chicanismo.

Chicano writers are often asked, "Are you a Chicano writer, or a writer who happens to be Chicano?" Women and other "ethnic" writers are asked the same thing. We believe that Tony was a Chicano writer—¡bien Chicano!—con safos y que!

But why us? What brought Daniel Chacón and Mimi Gladstein to dedicate themselves to the works of José Antonio Burciaga? We met when Daniel Chacón was being interviewed for a position in the Creative Writing Program at the University of Texas at El Paso. Gladstein was, at that time, associate dean of liberal arts, and she met with all the candidates for tenure-track positions in the English department. Chacón and Gladstein sat in her office as she questioned him about many things: his teaching, his own fiction, sample class assignments. Chacón answered each question like a job candidate. Years before, when she was chair of the English department, Gladstein had initiated the first bilingual creative writing class, taught by Ricardo Aguilar. She had also invited Arturo Islas to be a Distinguished Visiting Writer in the department for a year. She wanted to find out what Chacón knew about Chicano literature and so asked him what writers he would use if he were to teach such a class. He listed off names: Sandra Cisneros, Luis Valdez, Lorna Dee Cervantes, Ron Arias's *Road to Tamazunchale*. Suddenly, Gladstein leaned across her desk and asked, "What about Burciaga?"

Chacón exploded with excitement. "I love Burciaga!" he said and shared with her his experience of one of Tony's final readings. It had been at Delta College in Stockton, and Chacón had the privilege of reading with Burciaga in an auditorium full of Chicano students. That day Chacón, along with a handful of his students, hung out with Tony. Despite the fact that Burciaga was, by then, an icon of Chicano art and literature, he was gentle and humble. Chacón left Stockton that day loving not only the work, but also the man.

Gladstein shared with Chacón the special ties she had with Burciaga. She and Tony had been good friends since childhood. The synagogue in which he had grown up—where his father was the custodian—was her synagogue. Her mother and his father had often worked together, which Tony once wrote her made him feel "a familial relation." Tony regularly supplied her with Steinbeck material, as he knew that writer was one of her main research interests.

Our scheduled meeting was supposed to last a half hour. Forty-five minutes later we were still talking about Tony. We parted that day sharing something special, our love for Tony. As colleagues during the next four years, whenever we got together we found reason to mention Tony. Then one day, as we were eating dinner with a bunch of English department professors, Chacón leaned over the table and said to her, "What we need—what our students need—is the collected works of José Antonio Burciaga. Someday, I'd like to put together such a collection."

"That is a great idea, Chacóncito," Gladstein said. "I'd like to work with you on that project."

That was the seed. We could not let our respect for the man go unheeded. We had to honor him, and somehow we knew it was the right thing to do. Maybe it was the desert mountains around which we breathe, eat, write, and love, the same mountains that blew dust into the mouth of little Tony, sleeping in the basement of a synagogue. That earth, which all of us El Pasoans swallow on windy days, settled into his lungs and became part of his foundation as an artist and spiritual being.

A few months after our decision to honor his memory, we found ourselves in Carmel-by-the-Sea, at the home of Tony and Cecilia, in a basement with forty-one boxes and one empty chair. "Use whatever you want," Cecilia called from the top of the stairs. "We'll have dinner about seven."

That was the first day. We looked at the forty-one cardboard boxes. "I'll start with the prose," Gladstein said. She was especially interested in "The Temple Gang," Tony's memoir about growing up Chicano in a Jewish temple. He had written her about this work in progress; she knew many of the principal characters. Everyone who knows Tony's work can see how much he was influenced by Jewish culture and language. He often uses Yiddish words when talking about language. In "Pendejismo," he explains that where Spanish speakers would use the word *pendejo*, Yiddish speakers would say *putz*. "The Temple Gang" is the story of how he acquired that respect and appreciation for another culture, another belief. The sample we have included from this work in progress tells of how his father came to work in the synagogue and the birth of the "Temple Gang," his group of Catholic friends who hung out at the synagogue. There is even a vignette about seeing Jake Ehrlich, whose family belonged to the temple, and who was, before his death, the tallest man in the world. In these reminiscences Tony is at his best, at the fullness of his craft.

Chacón, looking down at the forty-one boxes, said, "I'll start with the art." As a young Chicano university student, he had read *Drink Cultura*, and it had helped to make him want to be a writer. He had often seen the cover image on T-shirts and posters, a green and red Coke logo that substitutes "Drink Cultura" for "Drink Coke." He had always admired one of the most famous murals in Chicano history, on the walls of Casa Zapata at Stanford University, *The Last Supper of Chicano Heroes*. He thought the fact that Tony chose Che as the "Jesus" figure at the center of the table made a lot of sense because Chicanismo was about self-identification and self-determination and Che represented that for many.

We spent the entire weekend in that basement, sometimes so excited about some poem or essay we found that one of us said to the other, "Listen to this," and we read aloud, Tony's words resonating within the basement. He was palpably present our whole visit.

One evening, Cecilia appeared in the door at the top of the stairs. We (and Tony) looked up at her. "I have a great idea," she said. "Let's get a bottle of wine and some cheese and crackers and watch the sunset from the beach before dinner." We left the house and walked a winding street through the houses of Carmel-by-the-Sea. Before his death in 1996, Tony had written about their home in the Carmel Highlands. "It's a marvelous fantasy . . . a dream come true." It *was* beautiful. Gladstein wished she had taken up Tony and Cecilia's many offers to come. "We look forward to your visit," Tony had written.

We came to the shore, a rocky precipice that overlooked the water and a rock formation jutting out of it. We came to an empty stone bench. The only thing on it was a doll, a Star Wars figurine some kid had left behind. Chacón picked it up. We all sat, staring at the water. Chacón sat the figurine, a little Luke Skywalker in robe and light saber, on the bench with us. We ate; we drank; we reminisced about Tony. As Gladstein looked out at the ocean, she felt it. Tony was with us. "It's going to be a great book," she said. We all nodded agreement. The little Luke Skywalker smiled. The waves slapped against the rocks.

CHACÓN *and* GLADSTEIN

PART ONE: *Cosas Lingüísticas*

Sanan llagas y no malas palabras.
Wounds heal, wounding words don't.

Hay quien mucho cacarea y nunca pone un huevo.
A lot of people cackle but never lay an egg.

La palabra vale lo que vale el que la dice.
A word is as good as the person who gives it.

Más hiere mala palabra que espada afilada.
A harsh word cuts deeper than a sharp sword.

Si de alguién te quieres vengar, has de callar.
Silence is the best revenge.

Vale más callar que locamente hablar.
It's better to say nothing than to say something stupid.

En boca cerrada no entran moscas.
Flies can't enter a closed mouth.

Bilingualism Isn't Just for Hispanics, You Know

*P*eople around the San Francisco Bay Area are familiar with the story about the two easterners who stopped at a gas station to ask for directions: "How do we get to Sanjosey?"

The attendant looked at them, figured they were from the East, and advised them, "Out west the *j* sounds like an *h*. It's not Sanjosey but San Hosay." The gas jockey then gave the two men directions and asked them where they were from and how long they would be in the area.

The driver of the car looked at the man and answered, "Oh, we just flew in from New Hersey, and we'll probably be here til Hune or Huly."

Governor Edmund G. Brown Jr. has urged all Californians to start learning Spanish. This request was followed up by futurologist Gerald Barney, who is editor of the Global 2000 report, a survey of world problems for the next twenty years.

My dreams never have been that ambitious. If people would at least learn to pronounce the Spanish names of people, streets, and towns in their own state, that would be a noble beginning.

When I first came to this state, I drove into Long Beach looking for San Pedro. Nobody had ever heard of such a place. Finally, one woman frowned at my question and said, "Oh, you mean Sanpeedro!" I had been mispronouncing it, according to some.

Years later, I went to San Francisco and was looking for Valencia Street. Again, nobody had ever heard of such a street. I was already late for my appointment when I spotted a mailman. "No such street," he said. "That's Mission over there, and that's Valencha Street two blocks that way." I cringed again.

It also took me awhile to decipher "Supple Veda" in Los Angeles. It's actually Sepulveda: "seh-pool-veh-da." And, of course, "Lossangeless" is actually pronounced "Los Anhejes."

There was a Latino TV news reporter in San Francisco who was fired from his job recently because he refused to pronounce "San Francisco" with an American accent. Soon after that, many TV and radio news reporters began pronouncing San Francisco the proper way. This was followed by city officials making it known officially that anyone calling the city by the bay "Frisco" would be frowned upon. The fired reporter did not get his job back.

Down the Bay Freeway from San Pancho (San Francisco), the San Jose City Council had been arguing whether their official stationery should have San Jose with an accent mark over the *e*. The outcome was lost in the fuss.

A fellow Texan came up to me one day in Southern California and asked me how to get to Sanclemeney. I looked at him with a question mark on my face. "Sanclemeney?" I asked.

"Yeah," he said, "yew know, where Wratchet lives."

"Wratchet who?" I asked.

"Wratchet Nixon, he lives in Sanclemeney."

I automatically switched to Texanese and showed him the way to Richard Nixon's San Clemente.

And so the battle against bilingual education continues by people who believe that only Hispanics benefit from it, oblivious to the fact that America's leadership role in this world is fast deteriorating because we refuse to learn other languages. It touches our very lives in the form of the national economy and national security. Why do we buy Sonys and Hondas?

Who and what are to blame? Our attitudes and the fact that high-ranking universities like Stanford do not have foreign language requirements either for entrance or for graduation with a BA degree.

According to a report issued by the President's Commission on Foreign

Language and International Studies, only 8 percent of U.S. colleges require a foreign language for admission, down from 34 percent in 1966.

Changes in Stanford's policy are being discussed, however, and the University of California system recently reinstated its foreign language requirement, which will be fully in effect in fall 1981.

An Anglicized Nightmare in Official English

*C*alifornia's Republican Senator S. I. Hayakawa is drafting a constitutional amendment declaring that the English language is the only official language of the United States.

The consequences could have no end.

I went to bed thinking about it and began to dream that all of the country's Spanish names of people, towns, and streets had to be anglicized.

I dreamt that the diehard Indo-Hispanic leaders reacted strongly against Senator Hayakawa's legislation. Nieves Palomares voiced his strong opposition, predicting that he would be a laughing stock if he had to change his name to Ice Cream Pigeon House.

Maria de la Luz Eterna, noted linguist, was quoted as saying, "Oh well, they never pronounced the names correctly anyway."

Texas, whose real pronunciation is "Tehas," claimed that its name is of American Indian origin. Nonetheless, it was expected to change its name to Taxes. Said the governor, "That's the way we pronounces it anyhow."

But not all Texans were happy about changing the name of their beloved monument, the Alamo, to Poplar. "'Remember the Poplar!' just doesn't have the same chutzpah—I mean pizzazz," said a city council member of San Antonio. The council member hoped to change San Antonio to San-tone. Said the mayor, "That's the way we pronounce it anyhow." English purists insisted on Saint Anthony.

In El Paso, militant feminists were strongly opposing the name change to The Pass, Taxes.

Amarillo, Texas, didn't think Yellow, Taxes, would be good for their image.

Soccoro, New Mexico, and Socorro, Texas (which translate to "Help"), were asking for help in naming one Help I and the other Help II. A Department of Interior official was quoted as saying, "If you help one, you gotta help the other too."

Arizonans were fuming over their proposed new state name of Arid Zone. The state chamber of commerce was proposing Air and Sun, but there was objection from the business segment because it sounded too much like Aaronson.

Californians still had not found a translation, but Governor Brown was going along with Hayakawa's proposed legislation even though last month he had been thinking of changing his name to Edmundo Cafe Hunior.

Residents living around Boca Raton were also reported to be very unhappy about changing their address to Rat's Mouth.

The small town of Aromas, California, had to change its name to Smells. Though Aromas is the same in English and Spanish, officials thought it might confuse people who thought it was Spanish.

San Francisco was ready to change its name to St. Francis out of respect for St. Francis of Assisi.

Yerba Buena officials claimed that changing the town's name to Good Grass or Good Weed would not help their battle against marijuana growers.

San Jose City Council members were complaining that their city's new name of St. Joseph would be longer and require more ink to print. They didn't know whether to use a period after "St." or not, and observed that there was already a St. Joseph in Missouri. Perhaps one could have the period.

Alameda de las Pulgas, a street that runs close to my home, was going to be changed to Flea Avenue.

That's when my dream got out of hand. The fleas were chasing me because I refused to change my name. General Alexander Haig was leading the fleas, telling them there were things still worth fighting for.

I awoke to learn with considerable relief that my name has not been changed to Joseph Anthony Abundance-of-Head.

Chicano Terms of Endearment

*W*hen I was growing up in El Chuco, better known as El Paso, everybody, every place, and every thing had a nickname. My brother was Pifas, our friends were Chuma, Big Del, Papo, Dos Equis, Mantenido, Rana, and so on.

We went to La Cate instead of Cathedral High School or La High instead of El Paso High. We crossed the border to JC, Juarílez, or Jarritos, but never Juárez. A bowl of chile was a *comunista* because it was red. We called chile *chilorio*. Tortillas were called "blankets."

Mexicans, Chicanos, and other Latinos have always had a special affinity for nicknames. It must be a tradition acquired from our indigenous ancestors who appropriately named persons, places, or things in relation to their reality and environment. José, Gloria, and James may be nice handles, but they seem generic when compared to Chufas, Big Del, or Macana.

Spanish and Mexican history is also filled with famous nicknames, from El Manco de Lepanto, alias Cervantes, to Tin Tan, Cantinflas, and El Piporro.

Back home there was always a reason to assign someone a nickname. For example, Henry Jiménez liked to hang out with the *batos*, carrying on and shuffling his feet instead of helping his working parents. His father would get angry and call him a *mantenido* (one who lives off someone else's earnings). So we began calling him Mantenido and eventually shortened it to a more respectable Monty. The girls always thought he had an amusing name until it was translated for them.

Monty got another nickname. One day, over a pitcher of beer, he was lamenting how his last name, Jiménez, was going to hold him back from success. "Had my name been Horowitz . . . ," he sighed. So, naturally, we began calling him Horowitz.

Fernando was another friend who had more than one nickname. Long before the beer of the same name was imported into the United States, we were calling him Dos Equis (two Xs) or just plain XX, because he was getting married for the second time. He had married too young, divorced too young, and at a still young age he was planning a second marriage.

Dos Equis also acquired a second nickname when he set up a fumigating business in El Paso. He became known as Matacucas, the cockroach killer.

Some nicknames were given by the family. Such was the case with Muggins, whose real name was Armando but some people called him Mogeens. Papo was another. Ray didn't particularly like the nickname his family had given him. When we found out, he was mortified. But last time I saw him, he introduced me to his son Papo, and gave me a challenging look.

Chuma was given that name because he began using a football helmet chinstrap that had CHUMA emblazoned across it. We also called him Schubert even though he was not at all musically inclined. Uva (grape) loved to drink wine. Rudy we called Rabbit, César we called Calixtro, and René we called Rana (frog).

"Savage" was more appropriate than "Reyes Moreno" ever was. In college, Savage could crush a glass or a thick glass ashtray or eat through a four-by-four wooden stop sign with his bare teeth in record time.

The de la Vega brothers became known as Big Del and Little Del. Big Del was also called Big Deal; Little Del was called Araña (spider). The Davis brothers were dark complexioned Chicano twins. One was a shade darker than the other, so one was called Día and the other Noche.

My brother Efraín was popular enough to have four nicknames: Pifas, Judas, Chapanecas, or just plain Chapo, which is short for short. I only rated one, Tónico.

Nicknames abound wherever Latinos live. In South Texas there lives a man they call Once, eleven, because as a child he constantly had a runny nose. He has a brother they call Doce, twelve. There are a couple of Chicano poets who are better known by their nicknames: Raúl Salinas, alias Tapón (plug), and Reimundo Pérez, alias Tigre. And of course everyone knows who Manos de Piedra is, or was. And the best pitcher around is Toro, alias Fernando Valenzuela.

Nicknames for women are not as common as they are for men. There has always been more respect shown for them.

Despite their sometimes teasing nature, nicknames in Latino cultures have always been terms of endearment. For in how many other cultures can you call a loved one Negrito, Gordo, or Flaca? Blacky, Fatty, or Skinny?

Por Quien Dobla la Campana—
For Whom the Bell Tolls

*L*ife," according to one Mexican ballad, "starts with a cry and ends with a cry."

The most popular folkloric figure in Mexican culture has been la Llorona—the Wailing Woman. In Latino culture, only women are supposed to cry.

"Los hombres no lloran"—men don't cry—is a phrase that brings memories to my tears if and when I ever do. I was raised to be a macho, but in the virtuous Mexican sense of the word, a gentleman with integrity, willing to respect and protect womanhood, *familia* and *honor*. In my culture *los machos no lloran*.

So if my Mexican culture frowned on men crying, my Anglo-American culture not only echoed the sentiment but further dictated that it was in very bad taste to display your emotions.

And so the times I've openly cried have been relatively few. I have choked up and repressed my tears more times than not. As a child I heard my father cry only once. It was a sunny Sunday afternoon in Mexico as our parents, aunts, and uncles sat around a kitchen table talking and laughing. While we were playing outside I heard the animated conversation turn to concerned voices and my father's with an emotional pitch. He was crying and kept repeating *en español*—"my children will never lack shoes." Everyone tried to assure him he had taken a joke too seriously. The shock of hearing him cry was healthy. It showed the love.

As a child, whenever I needed to cry I would go to a safe hiding place and not come out until my eyes were completely dry. Times that I cried include a terrible day as an adolescent when everything went wrong. It culminated with a soda machine taking my money and someone cheating me out of payment for artwork.

When my grandmother died. Once or twice when writing a poem. One memorable New Year's morning, hungover, I choked watching a parade of Walt Disney characters—the innocence of childhood. When I finished reading *Don Quixote*. When I discovered a Guatemalan Indian couple sleeping in a car in the freezing December of Northern California.

As a child I always thought that when my mother passed away it would be just like in the Mexican movies, à la Pedro Infante, Jorge Negrete, or Pedro Armendariz. I would go to some cantina, and cry, drink, and sing with mariachis. But as the oldest son I felt the responsibility to be the strong one, to soothe everyone else. I felt the same when Papá passed away. My wife and children thought I had formidable strength. Some pains are beyond tears.

Watching other people cry is painful, sometimes awkward; I will forever remember an older Spanish woman who literally drenched me with tears. I had been given the task of dismissing her from her job. More recently a woman friend called after finishing an investigative piece on the alarming high school dropout rate for Latinos. She was so drained and affected, and she tried to contain herself.

But emotional tears are good for us. Tears are supposed to be a normal biological reaction to rid the body of toxins that build up. Studies show that men who suppress emotions are more liable to suffer from stress-related diseases. The feminist movement and the gay movement should have taught us something. Crying is not a sign of weakness.

Twenty-five years ago, when President John F. Kennedy was assassinated, I was stationed in Spain. My two roommates and I sat and lay on our bunks, listening to the military cortege through the shortwave static and rolling drums. The announcer wept and described the scene. I too needed to cry like I have never wanted to cry before or again. But I had to stay still and suppress the need with all of my mind, body, and soul. How could I, a

Cielito Lindo. In an ironic use of the famous mariachi song ("¡Ay yay yay yay! Canta no llores"), Burciaga shows the sky is not so beautiful when full of war and destruction.

macho Chicano, begin crying when my two midwestern buddies remained so contained? Perhaps they too felt the same way. But my face burned and my eyes were dikes for the martyred president.

Life ends with tears and begins with tears. Whenever my mother heard of a birth, she would always pray loud, "Otro ser por quien llorar"—Another human for whom to cry.

Latinos have always known for whom the bell tolls. A communal people so used to adversity, we feel pain and rejoice with each other, for we know that it is in sharing that we have strength and unity.

Pendejismo

*M*ost popular Mexican cuss words begin with a *p*. Why words such as *pinchi*, *puto*, *político*, and *pendejo* carry such a harsh negative sound, I don't know. I'm not a linguist.

Pinchi, or *pinche*, is used to describe someone who is mean-spirited. The degree of insult depends on the intensity, the context, and who is delivering it. I don't know why the word is considered vulgar. In Spain, a pinche is a kitchen helper, and a few restaurants are named El Pinche, which many Mexican and Chicano tourists find hilarious.

Once when I was a kid, my big sister was angry and wanted to pinch me, so I said, "No pinching!" She ran to Mom and said, "Mamá! Antonio called me a pinchi!" Well, Mother, proper and educated woman that she was, gave me a tongue-lashing that I never forgot, and I could never convince her or my sister that what I had said was "No pinching!" To this day, my sister will only laugh and say she doesn't remember anything, but my ears still sting.

A *puta* is a whore in vulgar Spanish, as opposed to *prostituta* for prostitute. A *puto* is a homosexual.

Pendejo is probably the least offensive of these *p* words. In Guadalajara and some other parts of Mexico, it is a common everyday word. For the non-Spanish speaking, the word is pronounced "pen-deh-ho" (not "pen-day-hoe"); feminine, "pen-deh-ha"; plural "pendejas" or "pendejos." The noun, or committed act of a pendejo(a), is a *pendejada*. The verb is to *pendejear*. The term *pendejo* is commonly used outside of polite conversation and basically describes someone who is stupid or does something stupid. It's much stronger to call someone a pendejo than the standard Spanish *estúpido*. But be careful when calling someone a pendejo. Among friends it can be taken lightly, but for others it is better to be angry enough to back it up. Ironically, the Yiddish word for pendejo is a *putz*, which means the same thing.

In high school I had a friend whose name I consistently forgot. After I had asked him for the umpteenth time, he finally yelled, "Olivas! Pendejo!" So I called him Olivas Pendejo. At that same high school, we had a principal, Brother Alphonsus, whose favorite proverb was a reminder to students: "Naces pendejo, mueres pendejo!"—You were born a pendejo, you will die a pendejo.

Proverbs on pendejos abound in Mexican culture: Children say what they are doing, old people recall what they did, and pendejos say what they're going to do. Dogs open their eyes in fifteen days; pendejos never do. Of lovers that live far away from each other it is said, "Amor de lejos, amor de pendejos"—Love from afar, love for pendejos. The word can also be used to relieve pain: "No hay pena que dure veinte años ni pendejo que la aguante"— There is no pain that lasts twenty years nor a pendejo that will endure it.

El diccionario de la Real Academia de la lengua española (*Dictionary of the Royal Academy of the Spanish Language*) defines *pendejo* as a "pubic hair." The secondary definition of *pendejo* is "coward." Then there are tertiary definitions according to country: In Argentina, a pendejo is a boy who tries to act like an adult. In Colombia, El Salvador, and Chile, a pendejo is a fool or a cocaine dealer. There are a lot of those in this country. Here and in Mexico a pendejo is more likely to be a fool or an idiot.

Señor Armando Jimenez, author of *Picardía mexicana*, a collection of Mexican picaresque wit and wisdom, is also Mexico's foremost *pendejólogo* (pendejologist). According to don Armando, the number of pendejos, even as you read this, is innumerable. It has been estimated that if pendejos could fly, the skies would be darkened and we would enter a new ice age. The pendejos would get a severe sunburn. Some pendejos go so far as to believe that if all pendejos were to be corralled, there would be no one left to close the corral gates. That theory has been discounted by the fact that herding pendejos would be like herding cats. Pendejos have a mind of their own.

The great majority of people regardless of class, color, or creed are pendejos, according to señor Jiménez. His research studies claim that up to 90 percent of the world's population are pendejos. Of the remaining 10 percent, 5 percent are mentally unstable, 0.5 percent are geniuses, and 4 percent are unemployed—the exact amount needed for a sound economy. The remaining 0.5 percent are lost.

According to Jiménez, there are countless categories and types of pendejos. The following are but a few:

- The *políticos*, who think they will change the world with money, charisma, or speeches.

- The hopeless pendejos, who blame all their problems on bad luck instead of the fact that they are pendejos.

- The happy ones, who believe in their superiority over other pendejos who look up to them.

- The dramatic pendejos, who can be identified at a distance of one city block by their stance and by the way they walk, sometimes carrying a book or two.

- The pseudo-intellectuals, who act as if they are deep in thought on some theory when in reality they are wondering where they parked their cars.

- The optimistic pendejos, who are naive, happy, and talkative. They look for hidden treasures, mines, underground water. They also buy lottery tickets, bet on everything, and believe in television wrestling.

- The pessimistic or doubting pendejos, who don't believe anything you tell them. If you don't believe this, you fall into this category. And if you do believe this, then you might fall into the category of those pendejos who believe everything.

- Entrepreneurial pendejos, who have grandiose projects, are eloquent, and make great salesmen. If this type convinces you, you are an even bigger pendejo.

This list may be used for self-evaluation and to classify relatives, friends, and lovers. If you did not find yourself in any of these pendejo groups, congratulations! This means you're either a genius, unemployed, or mentally unstable. For those on the list there is still no known cure, but you are not to blame. Naces pendejo, mueres pendejo!

What's in a Spanish Name?

The first time I ever ran across a Spanish word in Anglo-American literature was in grade school when we were assigned to read Mark Twain's "The Celebrated Jumping Frog of Calaveras County." It was a fun-filled, humorous story. Despite my home-honed fluency en español, I did not recognize the Spanish word in the title and story.

I knew what a *calavera* was. It was a skull. For el Día de los Muertos in Mexico, there were little skulls made out of sugar and eaten like candy. In the Mexican game Lotería, La calavera was illustrated with the crossed bones under the skull.

But within the context of an Anglo-American English class, in a school where Spanish was strictly forbidden and punishable by paddling, ridicule, and writing "I shall not speak Spanish in school" a hundred times, the "Calaveras" of the story title was pronounced "kel-awe-ver-rahs." The Spanish word ca-la-ve-ras was hidden, disguised, nothing more than the name of a county. It was the mysterious name of an unknown person, place, or thing. Innocently or naively, I took the word to be just another eccentric English word pronounced with a suave Anglo-American accent.

It took me a few years to discover that Calaveras County in California had been named for Río Calaveras, where a great number of skulls and skeletons had been discovered by early Spanish explorers.

Like *calaveras*, hundreds of Spanish words remained in this country, changed, unchanged, and disguised due to loss of meaning, evolution of misspellings, and mispronunciations. After 1848, when the United States took over the Southwest, Spanish had to survive on its own.

There's a town in Texas named Buda. With a Texas accent it is pronounced Bew-da. On the highway from Austin (pronounced Awe-stn, or Ostin in Spanish) to San Marcos (pronounced Sanmar-cuss), there's a sign announcing Buda. That shouldn't have been odd, but being from Texas it just didn't seem right. I could have understood Buddha or even Buttocks, Texas, but Buda?

It didn't take much ask'n before learning that the name was originally Viuda, which is Spanish for "widow." Some monolingual Texan just didn't know any better and wrote it down the way he heard it. That's how we got *lariat* from *la rieta*, *hoosegow* from *juzgado*, and *buckaroo* from *vaquero*.

What's Polamas? That's a street in San Jose, California. It's actually supposed to be Palomas, pigeons, but the person doing the lettering on street signs just didn't know better.

The Bank of America put out some cute little refrigerator magnets the size of a business card for its Spanish-speaking clients where they could write important telephone "numberos." Numberos? That's neither English, Spanish, or Caló. The biggest bank in the U.S. of A. meant *números*. Even though it may have been an innocent bilingual typo, would you trust them with your *dinero*?

The one that has always troubled me is the English "tamale" pronounced "tah-mál-ee." The Spanish singular for this food item is *tamal*, plural *tamales*. Don't go to the English-language experts, because *Merriam-Webster's New Collegiate Dictionary* also misspells *tamale*, its etymological rationale being that it comes from the Aztec Nahuatl *tamalli*.

Sarape is another such word. *Webster's* says it's *serape*, but in the Spanish-speaking world everyone pronounces it and spells it as *sarape*. Look it up in an English-Spanish dictionary or a Spanish-English dictionary and it's *sarape* in Spanish and *serape* in English. Why?

Throughout the last century and a half Spanish has had free rein, running wild, with complete freedom to produce some mighty interesting words and sounds, not only from gringos but from Mexicans themselves.

Murrieta is now spelled "Murieta," Monterrey is now "Monterey," and Arrastradero is now "Arastradero." Why anyone decided to take away the rolling r from so many of the Spanish words is beyond *moi*. Did someone find the extra *r* unnecessary, were they in short supply of *r*'s, or was it just too difficult to roll their *r*'s in Spanish?

In addition, words from sixteenth-century Spanish still roam throughout the Southwest, along with caló, the Chicano dialect. These words have flourished and even emigrated back to Mexico where they have become part of the popular vernacular of the masses. The opposite also happens in Mexico and France and the rest of the world for that matter.

Though there may be many innocent reasons for this evolution of language, the isolation and syncretism, the fusion of two cultures in language, is fascinating.

I ran across a word in Mexico that is related to this argument but couldn't find in any dictionary, much less a synonym. It was *resemanticización*—resemanticization, also absent from an English dictionary.

Resemanticization was not defined, but it was derived from the word *semantics*—the historical and psychological study and classification of changes in the meaning of words or objects. In politics and cross-cultural situations, words, ideas, and objects constantly assimilate, "transculturate," or adapt for the sake of survival.

Thus the anglicization or hispanicization of words in this country. The word "Chicano" was a resemanticized term that was once pejorative. Alurista, an early Chicano poet, resemanticized many words, such as Aztlán, the ancient place of origin for the Aztecs that was and is the Southwest. Amerindio came to describe not only an "American" Indian but all indigenous peoples across the continent.

Chicano film, art, and literature constantly redefines, resemanticizes, an experience that is part Anglo, part español, part Mexicano. Resemanticization is also the exploitation of connotation and ambiguity in propaganda. Resemanticization deals not only with words but with ideas and symbols that cross borders and languages to take different meanings.

We become chameleons, we are chameleon. As we move from one world to the other we exchange colors, ideas, symbols, and words in order to fit, to relate, and to survive. The result is a prismatic iridescence when the differences of colors play on each other, like a rainbow after a rainstorm in the desert. We are chameleons.

Bullcycle. In one of his more whimsical moods, Burciaga came up with this etching, a visual word pun.

¡Ay Caramba!

"Caramba! Arriba! Arriba!" Speedy Gonzalez screams in a high-pitched voice as he slips, slides, and runs from one cartoon escapade to another. When Donald Duck travels South of the Border, he expresses his frustration with a "Caramba!" In Berkeley, California, there is a Mexican restaurant named Ay Caramba! Harmless enough, *caramba* is an interjection used to express surprise, amazement, or a little anger. It can be as mild as saying "Goodness!" or "Good Heavens!"

But *caramba* is a synonym for the root word *carajo*, and in the supposed bible of the Royal Academy of the Spanish Language, *El diccionario de la Real Academia de la lengua española*, a carajo is a penis, "the virile member of the male," and what Speedy Gonzalez is really saying is "Penis! Up! Up!" And, the restaurant name translates to "Oh, Penis!"

Another synonym for *carajo* is *caray! Caray* and *caramba* are mildly disguised synonyms for the word *carajo*, which has many rich and varied meanings. But *El diccionario de la Real Academia de la lengua española* claims only this definition for *carajo*: "The virile member of the male. A bad sounding interjection."

In a short story I used the word *carajo*. The story was selected for a high school literature anthology, but not before receiving a letter from the permissions editor who wanted to censor *carajo*. "Some teachers objected to it," she wrote. Instead of *carajo* could they use the word *idiota*? How they substituted *idiota* from *carajo* was a mystery until I discovered it was just one of many definitions for *carajo*.

Few Latinos, except for the authors of the *Royal Dictionary*, call their penis a carajo. Like most other español-speaking folk, my use of "Carajo!" was to express amazement and surprise. Like so many other people that use "Carajo! caray!" And "Caramba!"

No! I wrote back to the permissions editor. You may not change *carajo!* to *idiota!* I explained and gave her an alternative: "If you do not want to use *carajo*, you may substitute *caray* for *carajo*. But not "Caramba!" "Caramba!" is too much like "Gee whiz!" That's why Speedy Gonzalez and Donald Duck use it.

Carajo also means tricky, mischievous, difficult, and hard to resolve. Of course, a carajo is all those things, but few Latinos ever make that relationship. The synonyms are endless, from *caracho*, *caray*, and *carraspirina* to *baramba*, *baray*, and *carajo*.

The sometimes ignorant power of the Royal Academy of the Spanish Language angered if not amazed many Latin American writers because the word *carajo* was forbidden from the *Diccionario de la Real Academia* until the 1987 edition.

In *El diccionario de mejicanismos*, Francisco J. Sanatamaría assailed the powerful Royal Academy for not permitting the word *carajo* a definition in the dictionary, "that 'sublime interjection,' the most expressive in our language. And what are the reasons for its dismissal? Because it is a vulgar word, some say. Disgraceful the language that only has words for the tame and the ladies. . . . A language should be a palette where all social classes, ignorant or distinguished, may find a color to their satisfaction in order to express their ideas and passions, giving life and color to all concepts."

The etymology of the word *carajo* is old and thus long and complex, and uncertain. In his *Diccionario secreto*, Camilo José Cela notes the word could have come from the Latin vulgate *characulus* that gave birth to *caraculum*, *carere*, to copulate. That *characulus* could have originally come from the Greek *karakallón*. Cela gives many possible origins to the word, including the observation that *carajo* has *cara*, "face," and *ajo*, "garlic," and how one poet used *cara de ajo* to suggest a penis. In Spain, *hechar ajos*—to throw garlic—is a pun that translates to throwing carajos. Carajo is also used to invalidate worth, *no vale un carajo*—it's not worth a carajo. To send someone *al carajo* is to send him or her to a distant place, such as hell. The *Secret Dictionary* quotes various ancient erotic poems that utilize carajo as a phallic symbol.

According to this clandestine dictionary, even the word *cariño*, one of the most beautiful Spanish words, which translates to affection and love, originally came from *carajo*.

In Mexico and the United States, *¡carajo!* is a mild interjection when compared to the awe-mighty Mexican word *chingado*. And, *chingado* has its own mildly disguised synonyms such as *¡chihuahua!* or *chinelas*.

Though *chingado* is considered a vulgar word, it can be used ad infinitum, in a variety of ways, positively or negatively, from the basic *chignón* to *chingonométrico* depending on the context and intonation. But that's a whole other word and there is a whole book on that one word, entitled *El Chingolés!*

¡Caramba!

Bilingual Cognates

Bilingual Love Poem

Your sonrisa is a sunrise
that was reaped from your smile
sowed from a semilla
into the sol of your soul
with an ardent pasión,
passion ardiente,
sizzling in a mar de amar
where more is amor,
in a sea of sí
filled with the sal of salt
in the saliva of the saliva
that gives sed but is never sad.

Two tongues that come together
is not a French kiss
but bilingual love.

A cognate is a word related to another through derivation, borrowing, or descent. From one language to another, I suppose they become bilingual cognates if not bloopers. Like in the poem above, there are Spanish and English words that look alike or sound alike:

- Vincent Price has been known as "beans and rice" or vice versa.

- El Benny Lechero was actually a short serial movie character in the fifties known as "The Vanishing Shadow."

- Somewhere in the Southwest there was a teacher who thought his Chicano kids were calling him "Cool Arrow" when in reality they were calling him a *culero*, an insult.

- Two Chicanos were dining at a fashionable restaurant, and one of them says to the other. "This is the best *gabacho* (gazpacho) soup I've ever tasted."

- My mother once called her comadre, and the woman's German-born husband answered. "Lucina is not in," he said in perfect Spanish, "she is out buying *grocerías*." (*Groserías* are coarse, vulgar statements and acts.)

- One morning our friend Muggins called and my mother answered. Trying to be courteous, he asked my mother in Spanish how she was born instead of how she had awakened: "Buenos días, señora. ¿Cómo nació?" instead of "¿Cómo amaneció?"

Some are not necessarily cognates, but the mental mistranslations sometimes result in funny situations. My friend Rana has forever confused his Spanish with his English. As a high schooler, he was dazzled by a beautiful young woman and greeted her with "How are you going?" from "Cómo te va?" Even in English he had trouble. Lone Star Beer became "Long Star," humble became "noble," and misconstrue became "misconstrew." In the context of a serious conversation the result is laughter.

Jokes abound about Latinos who come to this country and read English signs in Spanish. Back when Cokes were only a dime, a Mexicano put a ten-cent coin in the machine but did not receive a bottle of Coke. He waited, hit it, and nothing. Finally he read just above the coin slot where it said "Dime" (which translates to "tell me" in Spanish). So he bent down to the slot and whispered into it, "Dame una Coca-Cola."

We have all seen real estate signs that say "For Sale, No Lease." A newly arrived immigrant looking for housing read the sign and kicked the door open. If you read that in Spanish and run the first two words together, it reads, "Force it, it's all right."

Introducing someone in Spanish is not the same as introducing someone in English. *Introducir* in Spanish means "to put in, to infiltrate." The correct term is *presentar*. Yet *introducir* is used so often that people don't even catch it. Many bilingual cognates have returned to Mexico to become part of what is known as Mexican caló. *Chansa* comes from chance, for *oportunidades*. *Trakes* for tracks, *mechas* for matches, *chutear* for shooting, *raides* from rides. Mexican film actor Tin Tan and singer Juan Gabriel have been very influential in "introducing" Chicano terms to Mexico.

Most of the Spanish terminology for baseball comes from English. "Ni ketcha, ni pitcha, ni deja batear" is a well-known proverb for someone who won't do anything and won't let anyone else do anything—He/she won't catch, doesn't pitch, and won't let anyone bat.

One of my favorite anecdotes is the one about my good friend and ex-roommate Darío Prieto. Though it has little to do with cognates, it shows how our bilingual minds sometimes work. At a Washington DC reception, he was once asked by our other roommate Ed Gutierrez, "Hey Darío, where does the Lone Ranger take his trash?" Darío didn't know, so Ed sang him the answer to the tune of the television show's theme: "To the dump, to the dump, to the dump! dump! dump! . . ."

Darío laughed heartily and then went to ask a couple the same question. But Darío always had to polish his English. He cleared his throat, something he always did, and asked, "Where does the Lone Ranger dispose of his debris?" The couple didn't know, so Darío sang the answer: "Ta-da-da, ta-da-da, ta-da-da-da-da . . ." The couple just stared at him.

Spanish Words in Anglo-American Literature

A Chicano Perspective

*W*illiam Sydney Porter (1862–1910), better known as O. Henry, was one of the country's most gifted and prolific story writers. Originally from Greensboro, North Carolina, he spent a good number of years in Texas, where he easily picked up the Spanish language, first from Mexican Americans on ranches and then formally through a Spanish book of grammar. According to E. Hudson Long, author of *O. Henry, The Man and His Work*, Porter knew "Spanish, English, and the Mexican dialect, known to Texans as 'Greaser.'" According to this Anglo-American friend, Porter knew a better brand of Spanish than the "descendants of Montezuma." And more than anyone before him, O. Henry used Spanish in his stories about the frontier country.

O. Henry's most famous character became the Cisco Kid, because of a television show based on this character from the short story "Heart of the West." Whereas in O. Henry's story, the Cisco Kid is a murderous outlaw, in the television series he is a good guy, a hero, with Pancho as his sidekick, reminiscent of Don Quixote's companion Sancho Panza. This story is filled with Spanish: The Cisco Kid, who at twenty-five years of age has already killed six men, has a woman friend by the name of Tonia Perez (most probably *Tona*, from *Antonia*), who lives in a jacal—shack— between *Frio* and the *Rio Grande*. Cisco is a bad *hombre* who killed because he was quick-tempered, to avoid arrest, or for his own amusement. His horse knows every *mesquite* from *San Antonio* to *Matamoros*. Tonia lives with her grandfather, who is in a continuous dream from drinking *mezcal*. There are many other *desperados*, and the people usually hid them or said *quien sabe* as they feigned ignorance of their whereabouts. Tonia has the fire and charm she inherited from the *gítanos* of the Basque Provinces. She also has a *chivo* she feeds from a bottle and sings sad *canciones de amor*. The story continues, filled with other Spanish words such as *pantalones, camisa, tienda, frijoles, El Chuvato Gregorio, lavandera, muy caballero,* and "*ay Dios.*"

Even though O. Henry's use of Spanish words is wide, he is also author of perhaps the most derisive literary work on Mexicanos, a poem published in *Rolling Stones*:

Tamales

This is the Mexican
Don José Calderon
One of God's countrymen.
Land of the buzzard.
Cheap silver dollar, and
Cacti and murderers.
Why has he left his land
Land of the lazy man,
Land of the pulque
Land of the bull fight,
Fleas and revolution.

This is the reason,
Hark to the wherefore;
Listen and tremble.
One of his ancestors,
Ancient and garlicky,
Probably grandfather,
Died with his boots on.
Killed by the Texans,
At San Jacinto.
Died without benefit
Of priest or clergy;

Died of mini balls,
Mescal and pepper.

Don José Calderon
Heard of the tragedy.
Heard of it, thought of it,
Vowed a deep vengeance;
Vowed retribution
On the Americans,
Murderous gringos,
Especially Texans.
"Valga me Dios! que
Ladrones, diablos,
Matadores, mentidores,
Caraccos y perros,
Voy a matarles,
Con solos mis manos,
Toditas sin falta."
Thus swore the Hidalgo
Don José Calderon.
. . .

The poem continues to tell the story of how Calderon vows retribution on the "murderous gringos" for the killing of his grandfather—metaphorically speaking, retribution for the Mexican ancestors killed in the battle of San Antonio after the fall of the Alamo—by selling, to "innocent purchasers" tamales "made of rat terrier, / Spitz dog and poodle, / Maltese cat, boarding house / Steak and red pepper." He ends the poem with:

This is your deep revenge,
You have greased all of us,
Greased a whole nation
With your Tamales,
Don Jose Calderon,
Santos Esperition,
Vincente Camillo,
Quintana de Rios,
De Rosa y Ribera.

This poem has been reprinted above exactly and complete with misspellings and missing accent marks as it appears in the 1917 Doubleday, Page and Company edition. Some of the misspellings indicate a direct derivation from English words, such as *Vincente* from Vincent.

From 1930 to 1940, Marcienne Rocard writes, "The yoke of the stereotype loosens." The usage of Spanish gets better, but there are still numerous instances or innuendos of typecasting Mexicanos. The treatment of the Mexican is still less than the treatment of the Spanish. The O. Henry "Tamales" poem is more reflective of the popular racist sentiments of the day in Texas than that found in other Anglo-American literature.

The distinction that Anglo-American authors make between Spanish speakers of Mexican ancestry and peninsular Spanish speakers is very marked even into the modern period. This difference is of particular interest in the modern period with Ernest Hemingway, another renowned Anglo-American author.

Lo del Corazón

Lo del corazón,
is that which comes from the Heart.
   Co-ra-zón
   pronounced ko-da-son,
   without the bow in the Ko,
      pronounced with a soft "d" and
         "son" instead of "zone,"
      with an accent on the són.
         Now repeat as you read:
         "Corazón!"
         Also pronounced Corathón
            in Hithpania.

            But in Aztlán
            you can say
cora   which is short for corazón

or you can say corazonsote
   which is very big hearted
      or a sweet and short corazonsito

   Literally and biologically
      it is the organ of circulation,
         that which is the ticker,
            the soul, the spirit
               or the gut feeling.
                  Lo del mero corazón
                    comes from the
core,   comes from
the center,   it is the
nucleus,   it is
the seed,
   it is the essence,
      and the quintessence.

   A corazonaso can be:
      a dolor de corazón—heartache
      corazón partido—heart break
         corazón doloroso—heart-rending

   Del mero corazón is:
      that which comes from a bottomless heart,
         that which gives love,
            that which gives valor,
            that which supports the backbone,
              that which gives nerve
              that which makes you love.

Love = amor
yo amo = tu amas
él, ella ama = nosotros amamos
   vosotros amais = ellos aman,
      Amén.

Modismos

DICHO: Del rico no apesta nada.
TRANSLATION: The rich do not stink.
APPLICATION: Apply cologne, aftershave lotion, or Chanel No. 5 when asking for a loan.

DICHO: Juntos pero no revueltos.
TRANSLATION: Together but not mixed.
APPLICATION: When ordering two eggs sunny-side up. Does not apply to bilinguals, biculturals, and bisexuals.

DICHO: Él que ríe de último, ríe mejor.
TRANSLATION: He who laughs last, laughs best.
APPLICATION: When told a joke, hold laughter to the last and have the best laugh.

DICHO: Lo mío es mío y lo tuyo también.
TRANSLATION: What's mine is mine and what's yours is mine too.
APPLICATION: Applies to the IRS.

DICHO: La necesidad desconoce fronteras.
TRANSLATION: Necessity knows no frontiers.
APPLICATION: Self-explanatory except to la migra.

DICHO: Roma no se hizo en un día.
TRANSLATION: Rome was not built in a day.
APPLICATION: Does not apply to Roma, Texas, built in twenty-three hours.

DICHO: A cual tierra fueres, haz lo que vieres.
TRANSLATION: When in Rome, do as the Romans do.
APPLICATION: In Roma, Texas, people do as they please.

DICHO: El cancer entra por una uña.
TRANSLATION: Cancer enters through one fingernail.
APPLICATION: Take no chances; trim all your fingernails.

DICHO: El dinero es la perdición del hombre.
TRANSLATION: Money is the root of all evil.
APPLICATION: Do not use money. Use checks, Visa, American Express, or Mastercharge.

DICHO: El panteón está lleno de limpios, tragones y valientes.
TRANSLATION: The cemetery is full of clean people, gluttons, and brave people.
APPLICATION: Be dirty, anemic, cowardly, and live longer.

DICHO: Él que a dos amos sirve, queda mal con uno.
TRANSLATION: He who serves two masters disappoints one of them.
APPLICATION: Does not apply to Mexican Americans, alias Chicanos.

DICHO: Él que no sabe es como él que no ve.
TRANSLATION: He who does not know is like the one who does not see.
APPLICATION: He who knows and sees is nosy.

DICHO: Él que no arriesga no cruza el río.
TRANSLATION: He who does not risk, does not cross the river
APPLICATION: The river is easy; life in this country is hard.

Colors Have No Translations

Green grows the grass
On this side of the fence
Barb wired river dance
Supple moons caress those moving hills

And deliver us your poor
And track them down in green army clothes
And arrest the earth that moves from under
And keep your green astro turf clean

Green that I hate you green
Green dollar backs
Green my bile
Green intentions
Green solutions
Green felt table top
Green Green
Green that I hate you Green

Green was my spring
Green were my crops
        In Green I trust
        Green that I hate you greed
        Greed Greed
        Greed your Greed
        Greed
        Green greed green creed
        Green that I hate you green

PART TWO: *Cartoons*

Editor's note: Burciaga created political/cultural cartoons under the pseudonym of El Indio Hispanic, the name itself a political commentary, citing the tension between those who self-identify as Hispanic and those who call themselves indios, Chicanos, "confused and full of rage" as Culture Clash would joke, the Chicano comedy troupe to which Burciaga once belonged. Many of his cartoons were syndicated through Hispanic Link and appeared in newspapers and magazines across the United States. We have collected a few of them for this volume, most of which have appeared in major U.S. newspapers. Some of these cartoons may be familiar to the reader, who perhaps did not know as they cut them out of newspapers and magazines, that Burciaga was the artist. Although they are humorous, they speak of the fundamental issues important to the Chicano community.

Lowrider. Rasquache is an aesthetic of Chicano art that uses whatever is available as the subject and medium of art. Here the artist humorously suggests that even the style of lowriding comes from necessity, from people stealing the back tires and backseat from some Chicano guy's car, making the first lowrider.

Bilingual Texan. Here the artist points out the irony of Texans demanding an end to bilingual education when the language they speak may not exactly reflect pure English, and may in fact be difficult to understand by those outside of Texas.

Los Changing Times. Notice the "Los" in the title. Linguistic and culinary mixing of cultures is a favorite subject of Burciaga. What would he have thought about the low-carb tortilla or the cultural shift from calling something a burrito to calling it a "wrap"?

Hispanic Unity Meeting. Oftentimes in political movements and associations, we fight among ourselves, commonly over small differences. Here Burciaga makes fun of the Hispanic unity movement, how the different ethnic groups fight with one another or stereotype other groups.

I personally prefer the post-pachuco renaissance...

Post-Pachuco Renaissance. The pachuco was an aesthetic subject for early Chicano art, especially with artists such as José Montoya. However, there has been a movement away from that, because many thought it was an idealization of street life. Burciaga humorously gives it a name.

Hungry Martians Want Mexican Food. Burciaga again uses food to make a humorous point about being Chicano/a. Here he combines the cliché of aliens asking "Take us to your leader" with the experience of Chicanos being asked by Anglos, "Where can I get the best Mexican food?"

Chicano Phone Call. The term "Chicano," as well as the lifestyle, is sometimes thought to connote lower social status. Even people within the community find the safest word for self-identification—the least threatening, the more mainstream—to be "Hispanic," a term created by the U.S. government for census purposes. Every Chicano knows it's easier to be Hispanic.

Chicano Dog. In Spanish the sound *wow* cannot be expressed with a *w* because it doesn't exist; so it becomes *güau*. Even though the sound is the same, the ways we think of it being expressed identifies us. Notice that the Chicano dog uses both, because he is a mixture of two cultures, and also notice his *Grrr*, the growl. The Chicano dog has attitude. Don't mess with him, *Grrr*...

PART THREE: *Las Fronteras of Culture Clash*

La cultura cura la locura.
Culture cures craziness.

Los locos y los refranes nos dicen las cosas reales.
Fools and proverbs tell us the truth.

Bueno aconsejar, major remediar.
It's okay to give advice about problems, but it's better to solve them.

Quien no oye consejo, no llega a viejo.
A person who won't take advice won't live long enough to give any.

Juntos pero no revueltos.
Together but not mixed.

El que sirve a dos amos, no queda bien con ninguno.
Who serves two masters, disappoints both of them.

Después de que una persona hace su marca en el mundo, llegan otros con un borreador.
After a person makes his mark in this world, people will arrive with an eraser.

Living Astride the Line between Two Cultures Can Be Difficult

*I*n English we say, "The clock runs." In Spanish we say, "El reloj anda." The clock walks.

In English we say, "I missed the bus." In Spanish we say, "Me dejó el camión." The bus left me.

In English we blame ourselves, and in Spanish we blame the inanimate bus.

Which is better? Which is right?

The assumption has generally been, here in the United States, that the English was always right. That's why, until recently, even educators used the term "culturally deprived" to describe citizens like me, of Indo-Hispanic heritage.

Until it was proved that intelligence quotient tests were culturally biased, many of us were accused of having low IQs, of being innately dumber.

Most tests are still culturally biased. I saw the word "hamper" in one recently. I never knew what that word meant until I was in my twenties. *En mi casa*, it was always "la ropa sucia," the dirty clothes, and in the military it is the "the dirty-laundry bag."

Now, we are cultural switch-hitters, able to function in two of them. The problem is that "culture" is one of the most misunderstood terms in this country.

Back home in Texas, I remember being told more than once by New Yorkers stationed at Fort Bliss that El Paso was a cultural desert. We had none, they told us. It took my departure from that bicultural oasis to realize that those New Yorkers were accustomed to buying *their* "culture" at a Broadway theater or at the Madison Square Garden. El Paso's culture was alien to them.

Culture is not a spectator sport that can be bought. It has to be lived.

Anglo-American culture has always been hard to define, perhaps because of its puritanical beginnings and the fact that we *norteamericanos* live in a goal-oriented, freedom-loving society.

It could be said that "the American way of life" is the American culture. Built around a strong work ethic and with an unending search for efficiency, we have adopted certain foods as national symbols—the hamburger, the hot dog. Dagwood sandwiches and french fries. We are obsessed with cars, television, movies, barbecue, and gadgets and more gadgets.

We Hispanic Americans are a culture-bound people because of the dominant culture. Just as IQ tests are culture-bound, so is housing, transportation, justice, health, and education. When behavior patterns and values do not assimilate into the dominant culture, you have cultural conflicts that express themselves through educational deficiencies, boycotts, demonstrations, riots, and crime.

Culture is the aesthetics, social experience, acquired manners, taste, speech, beliefs, actions, and artifacts of a people.

It is the strongest, most unifying aspect of Indo-Hispanic life. It is the sum of our attainments and learned behavior patterns expressing a traditional way of life. It can be gradually modified by succeeding generations. Thus we have Chicanos.

The Southwest, which is historically, sociologically, and linguistically Hispanic, Indian, Mexican, and Chicano, is a natural extension of the vast Latin American continent. It is incomprehensible to believe that everything north of el Rio Grande will be white and everything south will be brown. *Cafe con leche* (coffee with milk) can be very good.

Chicanos are a mixture of Anglo and Mexican values. The Mexican culture itself evolved from the Indian and the Spanish. The Spanish evolved from the Arabic, the Jewish, the Roman, and God knows who else. In mariachi music, one can hear the Arabic and Jewish mixed with the Indian rhythm.

To understand our two cultures is to understand two different meanings of time (the clock), language (the bus), and thought.

In Spanish we say, "Yo te amo." Which translates, "I, you love."

Chicanos have come out with interesting bilingual modifications that are fascinating to sociolinguistic students.

If our culture has been our damnation, it has also been our salvation.

The First Thanksgiving

I used to think Thanksgiving was one of the most cherished holidays this country has. The least commercialized, it is the one day of the year when we give thanks to the Almighty for His many blessings. The holiday calls up many memories.

I was nine years old. My brother and I played with our friends one brisk cold November afternoon. As the sun began to set, our friends went home to eat turkey, pumpkin pie, and all the trimmings. My brother and I went home expecting the same. We sat down at the kitchen table waiting for a feast. My mother put five bowls of freshly made beans before my brothers and sisters as she said in a quivering voice in Spanish, "Give thanks to God for having something to eat." We understood. My father worked that day and couldn't eat with us.

There are many versions of how Thanksgiving Day originated. Throughout their history, the indigenous people on this continent observed some form of corn harvest celebration. Popular tales have American Indians inviting the Pilgrims to join in the celebration. The Indians had taught the Pilgrims many survival skills and shared their food after the disastrous winter of 1620–21.

A favorite version is that the first Thanksgiving was a going-away party the Indians had thrown for the decimated Pilgrims, who were ready to go back. But after a bountiful harvest and a great party, they procrastinated and never left. That would be a nice version to believe.

William B. Newell, a Penobscot Indian and former chairman of the Department of Anthropology of the University of Connecticut, offers another story: the first official Thanksgiving Day was celebrated by white settlers following their successful attack on an Indian settlement when the Indians were conducting religious ceremonies. According to Newell:

> Thanksgiving Day was officially proclaimed by the governor of the Massachusetts Bay Colony in 1637 to commemorate the massacre of seven hundred men, women, and children who were celebrating their annual green corn dance in their own house.
>
> Gathered in this meeting place they were attacked by mercenaries, English and Dutch. The Indians were ordered from the building and as they came forth they were shot down. The rest were burned alive in the building. The very next day, the governor declared a Thanksgiving Day. For the next hundred years, every Thanksgiving ordained by a governor was to honor a bloody victory, thanking God that the battle had been won.

I prefer my fond memories and wish that I had never learned that last version. Or maybe it is better that we do know. The taste such painful history leaves on a day like Thanksgiving is especially acrid. But for that too we can say, Gracias.

Or we can believe that the first Thanksgiving was celebrated on April 30, 1598, on the banks of the Rio Grande, in the vicinity of what is now El Paso, Texas, years before the Pilgrims even landed on Plymouth Rock. On April 20, 1598, Juan de Oñate's expedition arrived from Mexico City at the Conchos River. Tortured by thirst and exhaustion, the group rested and recuperated. Ten days later on the 30th, Ascension Thursday, they celebrated with a solemn High Mass. Juan de Oñate naively took possession of the land in the name of His Catholic Majesty Phillip II and called it the Kingdom of New Mexico. A Capitan Farfán wrote and presented a comedy, a theatrical piece he had authored. This became the first Euro-American play presented in the United States. Of particular interest was Juan de Oñate's wife, who was the daughter of don Hernán Cortés and the great-granddaughter of Moctezuma. Señora de Oñate, a descendant of the two great leaders who clashed and merged to create a new race of Mexicanos and Chicanos, was not present but joined him later.

Or finally, we could believe that the first Thanksgiving was celebrated by the first indigenous people. Among the indigenous, Thanksgiving is not an annual celebration but a common everyday practice to request nourishment from Mother Earth and to give her thanks. You don't just take and give thanks afterward.

An Anglo, Jewish, Mexican Christmas

*T*he joys of the Yuletide season are double for bicultural children.

Mine were threefold. You see, I was raised in the basement of a Jewish synagogue, Congregation B'nai Zion, in El Paso, Texas, where my father was the janitor, electrician, plumber, carpenter, caterer, gardener, and Shabbat goy. *Shabbat goy* is Yiddish for a gentile who performs certain tasks on the Sabbath that are forbidden to Jews by Orthodox law, such as turning lights on and off. Every year, around Christmas, my father would take the menorah out of storage and polish it. This, for us, would signal the coming of Christmas.

The menorah is an eight-branched candelabrum that is symbolic of the celebration of Hanukkah. Hanukkah commemorates the first recorded war of liberation by any group of people. In 164 BC the Jewish people rebelled against Antiochus IV Ephiphanes, who had attempted to introduce pagan idols into the temple. When the temple was reconquered by the Jews, there was only one day's supply of oil for the eternal light in the temple. By a miracle, the oil lasted for eight days.

My father was not only in charge of polishing the menorah each year, but for forty years he also made sure that the eternal light remained lit in the temple.

As a child I was more in tune with Mexican Christmas celebrations, which at times came in conflict with Anglo-American traditions. Take for example the Christmas songs we learned in school. We learned about the twelve days of Christmas, and, though I never understood what a partridge was doing in a pear tree in the middle of December, I did like the melody. We also learned a German Christmas song about a boy named Tom and a bomb ("O Tannenbaum"). We even learned a Christmas song in the dead language of Latin, called "Adeste Fideles." Yet, although more than 75 percent of my schoolmates were Mexican American, we never sang one *canción de Navidad en español*. Spanish was not only frowned upon; it was forbidden.

Nonetheless, in our basement home, Mamá would teach us "Silent Night" in Spanish, night of peace, night of love. It was more beautiful, more romantic, and like a prayer in Spanish. There is an old saying about English being for business, French for love, and Spanish for God.

When traveling by bus, our American high school football team, made up mostly of Chicanos, would get into the spirit of Christmas and sing "Jingle Bells"; however, it always sounded like "Chingo Bells." For some reason, Brother Ambrose did not appreciate our version of that melody and upon hearing it would suddenly stop the old and dilapidated yellow school bus. Fortunately for us, we always wore our helmets and shoulder pads.

Outside of school we had our own little gang which we called the Temple Gang because we hung out around the shul or synagogue. One Christmas some of the gang decided they needed extra Christmas cash to celebrate in Juárez. Earning money was very hard for young Chicano high schoolers; the few jobs usually went to Anglo kids or the cheaper labor from across the border. So they decided to steal some Christmas trees and sell them.

Each of the four guys singled out a tree and ran. René had his eye on the most beautiful tree in the lot. At the proper time, Chayo, Chuma, and Rulis each grabbed a tree and ran. René grabbed his beautiful tree and tried to wrestle it away, but it just boomeranged and threw him to the ground. It was a real, live, planted tree.

René got up, grabbed the closest portable tree, and ran. It turned out to be the smallest and scrawniest tree we had ever seen. To add insult to injury, the next day he tried to sell it to a neighbor, who turned out to be the owner of the tree lot. René had forgotten to take the red tag off.

All three cultures, the Jewish, the Mexican, and the Anglo, came together during the *posadas*, which are celebrated for the nine days before Christmas. It is the reenactment of Joseph and Mary seeking shelter for the soon-to-be-born Baby Jesus.

This all began when my parents received a short and formal visit from their compadres Cruz and Elena Sánchez, who came to our home in the synagogue to ask my parents to be godparents to the Baby Jesus. So for nine days before Christmas we crossed the border into Juárez and took leftover candles from the Hanukkah celebrations to the posadas in a barrio in Juárez. We would pray and sing our Christmas carols in Spanish while playing with the melting wax on the Hanukkah-posada candles we all held in our hands.

After each Hanukkah service it is customary to give out fistfuls of candy, especially to the children. This candy, called *gelt*, consisted of chocolates covered in gold foil, like coins, and was given in small netted bags. My father would always be given some for his children, and it would wind up in Juárez for our traditional candy handouts after the posadas.

The next day we would be back at St. Patrick's Grade School singing "I'm Dreaming of a White Christmas."

One day I stopped dreaming of white Christmases in green forests as depicted by Christmas cards. An old Jewish immigrant from Israel taught me that Jesus Christ was born in desert country just like that of El Paso, my West Texas hometown.

E.T. and Me

*M*y six-year-old, Toño, finally convinced me to see *E.T.* The movie left an impression on me that few others have.

First, let me explain that I couldn't relate at all to the upper-middle-class Anglo kids who found E.T. behind their comfortable home. They ate too well, threw away candy, and wouldn't eat a pizza because it had been turned upside down in its box. The materialism throughout the house and in their trashcan was disturbing.

But I did relate to E.T., the funny little creature from outer space.

Physically, we are not all that similar. We are both shorter than the leading human being in the movie. But, based on my knowledge of E.T. and *Star Wars*'s R2D2, at five foot six I would be considered tall on most other planets.

E.T.'s nose is upturned. It exposes his nostrils for the world to see. I like to think that mine is a rather handsome nose, much like the nose of Tlaloc, the Aztec rain god.

E.T.'s skin is green. Mine turns green only after a night of drinking tequila. A bowl of red-hot menudo usually brings back my normal color—white. Yes, I'm white, not brown. I'm the white sheep of my family. But my face is spared from being lily white by the sun, eating lots of chile, and by character marks—acne, accidents, and actual fight scars—much like Richard Burton's character marks.

E.T. and the other movie star aliens from outer space do have a lot in common with me and other Indo-Hispanics, however, including illegal aliens.

All use nontraditional modes of transportation to get here. E.T. had his spaceship. I know of other illegal aliens who arrived in the trunks of automobiles, on water wings, in railroad refrigeration cars, or who were catapulted over the fence by friends using a teeter-totter-like contraption. They come in everything but adobe airplanes.

Generally, at first, all speak with an accent. And all show great ingenuity in avoiding uniformed bureaucrats.

The impression E.T. made on the kids in the movie reminded me of the impression I've made on people confronting a Chicano for the first time.

My earliest encounter was at a swimming pool not normally frequented by Mexican-American kids. Three blonde boys studied me from a distance before finally coming over to ask me if I was a pachuco. (You can only tell a pachuco by his style of dress or talk, not by swimming attire.) I said no, but they didn't believe me. They ran away yelling. "A pachuco! A pachuco!"

When I was serving in the U.S. Air Force in Europe, a young British lady was disappointed because I wasn't wearing a sombrero. Then there was the Icelandic gentleman in Reykjavik who demanded to know what tribe I belonged to. Rather than disappoint his fascination with my physiognomy, I told him I was Aztec. Since then, I have learned my Indian blood comes from the Zapotecs.

This fascination with people who do not look like "everyone else" is universal. A round-eyed, freckle-faced, red-haired Anglo or a brown-skinned, Mayan-featured Mexican would get the same reaction in Beijing.

But the only aliens most United Staters seem to like are extraterrestrials. The caresses E.T. received at the end of the movie hopefully carried the message to the audience that dark skin is just as soft, smooth, and sensuous as white skin.

The kinship we Indo-Hispanics feel for outer space beings is real. After watching *Star Wars*, José Montoya, artist, poet, and *general* of the very successful California cultural group the Royal Chicano Air Force, went so far as to give Chewbacca and R2D2 new Spanish identities, Chuy Baca and Arturito.

But our bond with extraterrestrials may be fleeting. It has happened in Hollywood already: aliens from outer space are taking the best jobs from unpatriotic Hispanic Americans.

Who knows where it'll happen next?

The White Gospel

*I*n the beginning was the word and the word was seized by the white man and the word was white and all who wrote were expected to write like a white man. All things said were through the white word and without the white word nothing was said. The white word shone in the darkness; but the darkness grasped it not.

There were prophets of color with red words, blue words, and yellow words. They came from the four winds to bear witness to the white word concerning the truth that all might believe the true word. It is the true word that enlightens every man and woman who comes into the world, regardless of color. The prophets of color were in the world and the world was made through them and the world knew them not. They came unto their own and the whites received them not.

But to as many as received them, they were given the power of truth. To those who believed in them: who were born not of wealth, nor of the will of bigotry, nor of the will of man, but the truth. And the words of color were made flesh and dwelt among us. And we saw the glory of multicolored words—glory of the begotten—full of grace, beauty, and truth.

The proliferation of white words failed and a call went forth for third-world perspectives from Asian, African, and Chicano scribes from across the land. But to hire any qualified scribe was not sufficient. Publishers sought scribes who espoused and practiced "white writing." "Color the words white, color your emotions white, bleach your words with Clorox. Leave your words soft and white," we were beckoned.

Prophets of color, writers of multicolored words, yearn to write in their own image and likeness, utilizing their own spirituality, their own culture, their own passion, their own control and empowerment. But this was not to be, for everyone knows the power of words is in the control of the white media.

Ivan Argüelles, a Berkeley poet, in an essay titled "White Writing" (*Caliban* 4 [1988]), writes: "Evocative, finely crafted, witty, urbane, sophisticated, occasionally troubling but always safe . . . as American as Madison Avenue, can sometimes be politically correct, but sanitized and safe and with only faint air-brushed innuendos of anger. White writing is meant to be polished, to glide over the tongue, to amuse, to be clear, intelligible and intelligent, to be thoughtful, balanced and beautiful, well conceived, cool, artful, smart, sometimes darker than we care to admit but never indiscreetly black, full of phrase and feeling. White writing is polite, and cannot HOWL . . ."

Ethnic writers who criticize or satirize from their cultural perspective may be branded as condescending, with a bitter attitude, by white editors. Cultural idiosyncrasies do not translate well in white writing. Bitterness, vehemence, and anger are not accepted in white publications, except by well-established white writers. Spanish surnames are constantly categorized, inflated, or deflated with high or low status.

White writing is practiced by graduates of English and creative writing departments and the hundreds of writing workshops. According to Juan Felipe Herrera, a Chicano poet, these are the workshops that validate, propagate, disseminate, award, and define what writing is to them. "There is a great white literary sequence that works against what we say," states Juan Felipe. He urges a frontal attack on these writing programs, on a literary theory that we do not necessarily fit into, on the "amigoization" of our culture, the tendency to Americanize and make our culture palatable to the mainstream, thus weakening our literature.

Those who have learned conformity in order to please their class peers, the expert, and teacher are usually the first to succeed very well. They are preservatives of white writing tradition, champions of the status quo, shedding any remnants of accents or influence from their old culture, except perhaps for a nostalgic description of the innocent past. They are opposed to evolution and change.

The oppression of multicultural writers is not just by the conservative white writers or editors but also by white writing progressives who assign and preach the moral issues of the day through white writers with white words while ethnic scribes are relegated to harmless stories. Serious pieces on international issues or on Central America are very rarely written by Latinos. Progressive magazines such as the *Nation*, *Mother Jones*, the *New Republic*, and other so-called progressive white magazines rarely seek out Chicano or Asian American writers. These "politically correct egalitarians" do not even bother to ask for our opinions.

Those Latino journalists, poets, and other creative writers who have succeeded in the white writing world mainstream by embracing conservative political and white literary canons have been turned into role models of what good Hispanic literature should be. There are some Chicano writers who may rightly call themselves Chicanos but frown on Chicanos who write with deep feelings on political matters. So that even the term "Chicano" no longer has the political commitment and connotation it once had. There are conservative Chicano writers and liberal Chicano writers.

The passion, emotion, and sometimes *rasquache* elements in Chicano aesthetics embarrasses the refined white writers. "Rasquacheness" is a Mexican term used to describe raw and unrefined persons or things. It was first applied to El Teatro Campesino's theater style and then to other Chicano art mediums.

It was this rasquache-ness that some suspect influenced the birth of postmodernism. Postmodernism has many definitions and styles, but that now refined element of what was once rasquache was born from the political urgency of minority ethnic peoples in this country. Once it was appropriated by white art, bleached, spruced up, and anointed by white editors and critics, it became acceptable. Another appropriated form of Chicano art has been southwestern symbols and images such as chiles and hearts, coyotes, and other Indian symbols. At times, they have been whitewashed to pastel-colored designs, forgoing the bright colors. "White writing," Ivan Argüelles writes, "is willfully ignorant of literary traditions." White writing workshops, arts councils, foundations, and endowment boards ignore the rich heritage of revolutionary art and literature of Chicanos.

Consider our past classic tradition of revolutionary poetry by Nicaragua's Rubén Darío; of the Nobel Prize-winning Chileno poet Pablo Neruda, fighting for justice with a pen; Diego Rivera, David Alfaro Siquieros, and Clemente Orozco, who expressed their revolutionary zeal with a brush. Consider another Nobel Prize winner, Gabriel García Márquez, and his social conscience novels. Yet, these writers are more palatable to mainstream sensibilities in this country because they do not hit so close to home; their "quaint magic realities" are removed from the ethnic boundaries imposed here, where "never is heard a discouraging word."

Ivan Argüelles writes of the connection between white writing and language, between white writing and life: the need to express "profound emotional experiences, in order to cope or deal with what writing is and what life and literature are not."

Truth and sincerity cannot be forged through white writing alone. Style is aesthetic expression with sincerity, grace, and naturalness. The style of white writing comes from a few institutionalized dominant sources with vested interests in preservation of their tradition.

What goes for creative writers goes for ethnic journalists who have very few outlets for their writings. Mexico City has about twelve daily newspapers. Xalapa, Veracruz, a very small but cultural town in Mexico has approximately eight daily newspapers. Washington DC, San Francisco, and Los Angeles have one or two daily newspapers; New York, three. One can begin to appreciate the difficulty and the reason for the lack of ethnic writers in these newspapers and the reason so few ethnic writers decide to enter a field that refuses to publish or hire them.

As a writer who never took a creative writing or journalism class, I am humbly aware of my limitations and accept my shortcomings, but I am also perplexed when my pieces are described by the "white world" as "mood pieces," "there's a voice there," or "an independent mind on the verge of creating a new genre of Chicano expression," or "he has a unique style unlike . . ." But all this is better than Chicano literary critic Charles M. Tatum, who described my early poetry as outrageous, scandalous in tone and content. "His *Restless Serpents* is an energetic collage of cool, jive, hip, pachuco language, fractured images and litanies."

Uruguayan writer Eduardo Galeano, in his essay "In Defense of the Word," defines literature in this way: "one writes out of a need to communicate and to commune with others, to denounce that which gives pain and to share that which gives happiness." One writes against one's solitude of others. One assumes that literature transmits knowledge and affects the behavior and language of those who read, thus helping us to know ourselves better and to save ourselves collectively. But "others" is too vague; and in times of crisis, times of definition, ambiguities may too closely resemble lies. One writes, in reality, for the people whose luck or misfortunate one identifies with—the hungry, the sleepless, the rebels, and the wretched of this earth—and the majority of them are illiterate. Among the literate minority, how many can afford to buy books? Is this a contradiction resolved by proclaiming that one writes for the facile abstraction known as the masses?

Galeano writes about "the good fortune and misfortune to belong to a tormented region of the world, Latin America, and to live in a historic period that is relentlessly oppressive." Aztlán, better known as the Southwest, is part of Latin America. The Southwestern culture with a specific cultural, architectural, culinary, and language history is more Indo-Hispanic than Anglo-Saxon. What is germane and indigenous to "Aztlán" has been cultivated by Indo-Hispanics and not by the white word. Chicano writers, a product of that cultivation and who have cultivated the Southwest, have been excluded from interpreting their heritage, hopes, and visions.

Galeano's essays are filled with gems against the white word, which he calls "the mass media." "As a means of revealing collective identity, art should be considered an article of prime necessity not luxury. . . . For the people whose identity has been shattered by the successive cultures of conquest, and whose merciless exploitation contributes to the functioning of the machinery of world capitalism, the system generates a 'mass culture.' Culture *for* the masses is a more precise description of this degraded art of the mass media, which manipulates consciousness, conceals it rather as a means of erasing or distorting it in order to impose ways of life and patterns of consumption which are widely disseminated through the mass media."

Galeano believes that the fate of Latin American writers is linked to the need for profound social transformations. Chicanos, Asian Americans, Afro-Americans, and American Indians share that linkage. For Chicanos, we are the northernmost link of America Latina, or as José Marti wrote, "from the belly of the beast."

"Literature as an effort to communicate fully, will continue to be blocked from the start, so long as misery and illiteracy exist, and so long as the possessors of power continue to carry out with impunity their policy of collective imbecilization, through the instruments of the mass media. . . . Our effectiveness depends on our capacity to be audacious and astute, clear and appealing. I would hope that we can create a language more fearless and beautiful than that used by conformist writers to greet the twilight."

Galeano's haunting question to America Latina readily echoes in this country: "How many writers and artists have never had the opportunity to recognize themselves as such?"

In the beginning was the truth, and when all else is said and done, the truth will remain and it won't necessarily be the white word.

Reasons to Celebrate
El Cinco de Mayo

*T*he U.S. Civil War might have turned out very differently had the French won the battle that Cinco de Mayo, 1862, in Puebla, Mexico. Had the French been victorious, they would have aided the South in the U.S. Civil War and our destiny might have been very different.

Justo Sierra, 1848–1912, a great Mexican writer and author of *The Political Evolution of the Mexican People*, made this observation at the turn of the century.

In 1861, Mexico was bankrupt, owing staggering sums to Britain, Spain, France, and the United States. Years earlier, the United States had offered to cover Mexico's debt in exchange for a mortgage on part of Mexico's territory. Having already lost half its territory to the United States, Mexico rejected the offer.

What kept the European powers from direct intervention in Mexico was the Monroe Doctrine of 1823, which prohibited Europe from interfering in this hemisphere.

But in the summer of 1861 the U.S. Civil War broke out, and in October, France, Spain, and England convened to sign the Covenant of London, agreeing to send troops to Mexico in sufficient numbers to secure payments. They solemnly added that this use of force was not for territorial gain or, ironically, to interfere in Mexico.

Spain and England sent the first bill-collecting expedition to Veracruz. Although the Europeans encountered no resistance and an agreement was reached, they didn't collect their money.

Meanwhile, France landed a sizable force, and the European intervention became exclusively French. On May 5, 1862, the French attacked Puebla, and a ragtag, poor and hungry, half Indian-Mexican army, under General Ignacio Zaragoza Seguín, beat the better-armed French forces, at that time the most powerful on earth. Zaragoza, ironically, was born in Goliad, Texas, when that state was under the Mexican flag.

The victory gave Mexico an electric current of patriotism and inspiration. It gave Mexico a soul of her own and national unity. This is perhaps one reason why el Cinco de Mayo is almost as important as September 16, Mexican Independence Day.

While the Cinco de Mayo battle raged, Robert E. Lee was winning battles for the South. Had France won at Puebla, it would have joined forces with the South and easily convinced England to help free the Southern ports from the Union blockade. Louisiana had at one time been French. France and England also wanted to halt U.S. expansion into Latin America. Napoleon III also dreamed of establishing stronger ties between France and Mexico, since both were Latin countries, and in the process gave birth to the term "Latin American."

The victory at Puebla not only protected the integrity of Mexico but also that of the United States—"an involuntary service . . . of inestimable value," Justo Sierra wrote in *The Political Evolution of the Mexican People*.

A year later the French won several victories, paving the way for Napoleon III to send Maximilian, the unemployed archduke of Austria, and his wife, Carlota, to set up a monarchy in Mexico. But the Mexican resistance persisted and Washington continued to recognize the Benito Juárez government as the only legitimate one. At times the Juárez government was situated in El Paso del Norte, now renamed Ciudad Juárez and across from El Paso, Texas. At times the Juárez government had to go into temporary exile across the Rio Grande in Franklin, Texas, now named El Paso, Texas.

Maximilian and Carlota set up their court, wrote a book on court etiquette, and reintroduced royal grandeur, first imported to Mexico City by Spain.

In 1865, the U.S. Civil War ended, and in 1866 armed resistance against the French occupation grew. The victorious U.S. Union army clamored for war against the French in Mexico. General Ulysses Grant declared it was necessary to aid the Republic of Mexico. Grant had already been to Mexico as part of the American invasion of 1847. For Mexico, the possibility of U.S. involvement was more frightening than the French presence. At the urging of the United States, the French departed, but also because they had their own problems in Europe.

So the United States inadvertently repaid Mexico for its help in keeping the French from becoming allies of the Confederates.

But Maximilian would not abdicate his throne, declaring he was 100 percent Mexican, heart and soul. Besides, Napoleon had promised to stand by him. Carlota had already returned to France to hold Napoleon to his word. Napoleon reneged.

Maximilian remained in Mexico and bravely met his execution on June 19, 1867. Carlota became despondent and eventually went insane. She died in Belgium in 1922.

Mexico's second war of independence ended with three hundred thousand casualties.

How did France influence Mexico? Mexican law is based on the Napoleonic Code, and Mexico's architecture was greatly influenced. Popular dances such as la Varsoviana are of French origin. Mexico's bread and pastries are of French origin. In Cuernavaca, the police are still called gendarmes. In Mexico City, el Paseo de las Reforma was Maximilian's idea of a direct route to his palace from the center of the city. It was modeled after the Champs-Élysées. (Contrary to popular belief, the French did not influence or institute mariachis.)

Had Mexico not won at Puebla, it is very possible that the South might have won the war and we might have had a different Mexico and a different United States. Thus we have every reason and right to celebrate. ¡Vive la différence! ¡Viva el Cinco de Mayo! ¡Viva México!

The Last Supper
of Chicano Heroes

*I*n 1988, I polled one hundred Chicano students at Stanford University
and one hundred Chicano activists from the late 1960s to find out
whom they considered the top thirteen Chicano heroes.

The idea arose from a mural that I was designing on the mythology and
history of *maíz*, corn. I had intended to depict the Last Supper; Christ
and his twelve apostles were to be portrayed eating tortillas, tamales, and
tequila instead of bread and wine. I dropped that idea when some students
expressed dismay at my mixing humor with religion. That's when I decided
to replace the religious figures with thirteen Chicano heroes. The mural,
now finished, is in the dining hall of Casa Zapata, the Chicano theme
student residence at Stanford University.

The survey was received positively and as a novelty, with a 70 percent
return.

The final thirteen Chicano heroes reflected the choice of the older activists because their votes were concentrated on a smaller group of heroes
who had played important parts in the Chicano Movement as activists or

symbolic historical figures. The students were more inclusive and offered a total of 240 hero candidates.

The selection process brought into question the very definition of a hero or heroine as a mythical, historical, symbolic, military, or popular cultural figure.

The first historical Chicano hero, according to some, was General Ignacio Zaragoza, born in Seguín, Texas, when Texas was part of Mexico. Zaragoza rose to command the ragtag Mexican army that defeated the French in Puebla on Cinco de Mayo, 1862. At that time, the French army of Napoleon III was the most powerful in the world. But Zaragoza did not make the final list. Nonetheless, he does stand behind the seated thirteen. One who did was a man who preceded him both in time and in popular lore, the California rebel Joaquín Murrieta.

Three Chicanos who started their careers together made the list: Cesar Chavez, Dolores Huerta, and Luis Valdez.

La Virgen de Guadalupe, patroness of Mexico, received enough votes to sit at the table but out of respect occupies a loftier place above the Chicano Last Supper. In a history mobbed with *machos*, there was a sincere effort to vote not only for women like Frida Kahlo and the poet sor Juana Inés de la Cruz but also for mothers and grandmothers.

Not all the heroes had to be Chicano—that is, of Mexican ancestry; thus Argentine-born, Cuban hero Ernesto "El Che" Guevara made the list. The martyred Che, a strong symbol during the Chicano Movement of the late sixties, occupies the central position because he was the most Christlike, with his beard, revolutionary idealism, and martyrdom. At his side is an earlier Mexican revolutionary, Emiliano Zapata.

Dr. Martin Luther King Jr. was another non-Chicano who made the last supper. The late president John F. Kennedy also received some votes but not enough to sit at the table. He is in the background, along with General Zaragoza and others who did not make the final list.

Carlos Santana, who helped revolutionize North American music with Latino sounds, stands and serenades the chosen thirteen.

Death received enough votes to stand behind the lucky thirteen. *La muerte*, so popular in Mexico, is a heroine, a great avenger and savior from *la vida*.

One student voted for Juan Valdez of the television coffee commercial, Jose Cuervo tequila, Speedy Gonzalez, señor Don Gato, Julio Iglesias, Pedro the Mexican Jumping Bean, Tattoo from *Fantasy Island*, Chiquita Banana, Menudo, and Zorro the Gay Blade. This list was at once humorous and revealing about how Latinos are sometimes perceived through stereotypes and media stars.

Last Supper of Chicano Heroes. This is one of the most famous images in Chicano art, a mural at La Casa Zapata at Stanford University.

Chicano heroes have always been an elusive lot. Mexicanos and Chicanos have traditionally frowned on the North American individualism that Alexis de Tocqueville described one hundred and fifty years ago. Most of Mexico's national heroes were martyrs, having died in service to the people—from Miguel Hidalgo, father of Mexican independence, who was excommunicated and executed, to revolutionary heroes Francisco Villa and Emiliano Zapata, who were ambushed and assassinated.

In the survey, the group-oriented focus came through time and again in votes for mothers, fathers, grandparents, Vietnam veterans, braceros, campesinos, and pachucos. But it was best expressed by a student who chose as his heroes, "all the people who died, scrubbed floors, wept, and fought so that I could be here at Stanford."

The Top Thirteen Chicano Heroes

1. Cesar Chavez—Founder and president of the United Farm Workers Union.

2. Emiliano Zapata—Mexican revolutionary hero.

3. Dolores Huerta—Founder and vice president of the United Farm Workers.

4. Frida Kahlo—Mexican painter, wife of Mexican muralist Diego Rivera.

5. Luis Valdez—Founder of El Teatro Campesino, playwright, and director of films such as *La Bamba* and *Zoot Suit*.

6. Ernesto "El Che" Guevara—Argentine-born hero of the Cuban revolution.

7. Joaquín Murrieta—Young California rebel/bandit who fought against Yankees.

8. Tomás Rivera—Chicano educator and writer.

9. Sor Juana Inés de la Cruz—fifteenth-century Mexican nun, poet, early feminist.

10. Dr. Martin Luther King Jr.—Civil rights leader who supported the farmworkers and inspired the Chicano Movement.

11. Benito Juárez—Mexican president, liberator. Contemporary of Abraham Lincoln.

12. Ricardo Flores Magón—Mexican revolutionary, writer, and intellectual.

13. Ernesto Galarza—Early Chicano activist, writer, poet, and Stanford graduate.

Pachucos
and the Taxicab Brigade

*T*hursday, June 3, 1943, was a warm inviting night for over fifty thousand military servicemen stationed around the Los Angeles area. Weekends began on Thursdays, and this particular Thursday was soon after payday.

That evening, a group of eleven sailors walked into the middle of a barrio along the 1700 block of North Main Street. According to their documented statement, they were attacked by a gang of young Mexicans. The sailors, who claimed they were outnumbered three to one, suffered minor cuts and bruises.

The incident was reported to a police station. There, some of the policemen formed a "vengeance squad" and set out to arrest the gang that had attacked the sailors. By the time they got to the scene there were no Mexicans or Mexican Americans. The police raid was a fiasco, and the only solution left was to report it to the newspapers, which in turn whipped up the community and the military against the Mexican population.

The next night, approximately two hundred sailors decided to take the law into their own hands by hiring a fleet of twenty taxicabs and cruising down the center of town toward East LA. The first victim of the "Taxicab Brigade" was a young Mexican "zoot suiter" who was left badly beaten and bleeding. The total tally for that night: two seventeen-year-olds, one nineteen-year-old, and one twenty-three-year old, all left on pavements or sidewalks for the ambulances to pick up. The police were unable or refused to intercept the Taxicab Brigade. It was just another punitive military expedition.

On June 4, the LA newspapers took a rest from the war news to play up the "Zoot Suit War," named after the zoot suits worn by Mexican-American youths. The local press adopted a just and righteous attitude on the part of the servicemen. On the following day, hundreds of soldiers and sailors paraded through downtown LA, warning zoot suiters to closet their drapes or suffer the consequences. LA police, shore patrol, and military police did nothing, apparently because of the number of frenzied service-men involved.

On June 7, civilians joined their military counterparts and mobbed restaurants, bars, and theaters in search of not only Mexicans but also "Negroes" and Filipinos.

The following is one eyewitness account by Al Waxman, editor of the *Eastside Journal*: "Four boys came out of a pool hall wearing the zoot suits. Police ordered them into arrest cars. One refused. . . . The police officer answered with three swift blows of the night-stick across the boy's head and he went down. As he lay sprawled, he was kicked in the face. Police had difficulty loading his body into the vehicle because he was one-legged and wore a wooden limb. . . .

"At the next corner, a Mexican mother cried out, 'Don't take my boy, he did nothing. He's only fifteen years old. . . .' She was struck across the jaw with a night-stick and almost dropped the two and half year old baby that was clinging in her arms. . . ."

Waxman witnessed several other incidents and pleaded with the local police station, but they answered, "It is a matter for the military police." The Mexican community was in turmoil. Mothers, fathers, sisters, aunts, and uncles swarmed police stations looking for their lost children.

By June 8, the LA district attorney declared "the situation is getting entirely out of hand." The mayor, however, thought matters would eventually blow over, and after a count of the Mexicans in jail, the chief of police thought the situation had cleared up.

But it was not over for the press. The *Los Angeles Times* stated the riots were having a "cleansing effect." A *Herald Express* editorial said the riots "promise to rid the community of . . . those zoot suited miscreants." Meanwhile, the "miscreant" military operations spread to the suburbs. The Los Angeles City Council adopted a resolution making the wearing of zoot suits a misdemeanor.

Finally, on the heels of a navy declaration that downtown LA was "out of bounds," and following the Mexican ambassador's formal inquiry to the U.S. Secretary of State, and other expressions of international concern, the *Los Angeles Times* took a conciliatory and pious tone, disassociating any possibility of bigotry from the riots. At the same time, the *Times* went on the offensive, attacking defenders Carey McWilliams and Eleanor Roosevelt for stirring up racial discord.

Similar "zoot suit" disturbances were reported in San Diego on June 9; in Philadelphia on June 10; in Chicago on June 15; and in Evansville, Indiana, on June 27. Bigotry-based riots also occurred in Detroit, Harlem, and Beaumont, Texas.

Relations with Mexicans and Mexican Americans had seemed warm and friendly up to that point. But those were only diplomatic relations. In 1941, a bracero program had been agreed upon and signed by the two countries, allowing Mexican farmworkers to work on this side, thus freeing U.S. field hands to work in defense industries or in the military. A month before the June 3 riots, Mexican soldiers had paraded through downtown Los Angeles in a Cinco de Mayo celebration. At the same time, Mexican and U.S. navies exchanged information on Japanese activities off the coast of Baja California.

The riots lasted for ten days, ending on June 13, 1943. Unlike modern riots, these were sporadic and scattered fights. No one was killed or sustained massive injuries. Property damages and convictions were minimal. And it was not the Mexican-American youth who rioted but the military. Carey McWilliams, author of *North from Mexico*, called them "government riots."

In *The Zoot-Suit Riots*, Mauricio Mazón, a history professor at the University of Southern California, wrote: "at least for ten days in Southern California . . . the military lost control of several thousand servicemen." Several archived military memos confirm the image of an impotent military brass. The frenzy was fed by the press, which predicted massive retaliations by Mexican zoot suiters.

There were no political manifestos or heroes originating from the riots— except for the pachucos, the first Mexican-American youths to rebel and strike their own self-identity through the zoot suit. To this day they live in literature, films, murals, dance, and historical accounts. They live, too, through their social and cultural descendants, the cholos.

The pachuco has enjoyed a cultural aura, complete with stylistic pathos. He was both a tragic and heroic figure—a mythical creation. El Pachuco is the preeminent Don Quixote of Aztlán (the mythical southwest where the Aztecs began their journey to found Tenochtitlan, today's Mexico City).

This powerful figure has captured the imagination of artists, writers, poets, and philosophers, including Nobel Prize winner Octavio Paz, who in 1950 devoted the first chapter of *Labyrinth of Solitude*, his classic study of the Mexicano character, to "El Pachuco and Other Extremes." Although Paz maligned the pachuco, he now recants and regrets that early analysis. His chapter offered a derisive condemnation of not only an adolescent caught between adulthood and youth but also caught between two countries, two vastly different cultures. The carefree adolescent years enjoyed by Anglo-American youths of the forties were nonexistent in Mexican culture. For Mexican youth, the age of fifteen became a rite of passage into adulthood, while young Mexican Americans chose to affirm a new identity.

A few years ago, Octavio Paz came to Stanford. At a dinner party my wife and I politely asked him for his views about Chicanos. "¡No sé!" he answered, refusing to touch the topic but attentive to our views.

Even before Paz's essay, Chilean author and Stanford University professor emeritus Fernando Alegría wrote the first known short story on el Pachuco in 1945, "¿A qué lado de la cortina?"

José Montoya, a Chicano multidisciplinary artist, poet, muralist, musician, and founder and general of Sacramento's RCAF (Royal Chicano Air Force, earlier known as the Rebel Chicano Air Force, earlier known as the Rebel Chicano Art Front), has concentrated many of his poetic, musical, and artistic works on el Pachuco. He lived the pachuco era, and his poem "El Louie" is a classic Chicano poem.

Luis Valdez's award-winning play and film *Zoot Suit* was the national debut for Edward James Olmos, who played the character of el Pachuco and whose black, zoot-suited image on posters elevated the zoot suit to the realm of an icon. Olmos then wrote, directed, and starred in the film *American Me*, which captures the Zoot Suit Riots of 1943 and follows the pachuco's descendants right down to the present-day cholos. The tragedy of urban Mexican-American youth has also been explored in *Stand and Deliver* and most recently *Bound by Honor*.

Within this cultural aura lies an important linguistic mystery: the origin of the term "pachuco." McWilliams suggests that the term came from Mexico and denoted resemblance to the gaily costumed people living in the town of Pachuca. He further suggests that it was first applied to border bandits in the vicinity of El Paso. Although McWilliams believes that the pachuco stereotype was born in LA, it was El Paso, Texas, better known as EPT or El Chuco, that had the reputation for the "meanest" pachucos.

Another little known theory is offered by San Jose State University professor emeritus Jorge Acevedo. As a conscientious objector, Acevedo resisted induction into World War II. For this action, he was sentenced to San Quentin but soon released to do community work as a counselor for braceros and homosexuals. Acevedo's theory is that the pachucos grew out of the repatriation program when more than 350,000 Mexicanos and Mexican Americans (the unofficial count among some historians is double that number) were deported to Mexico by the government during the Great Depression.

Acevedo recalls working through churches and social organizations to smuggle U.S. citizens of Mexican descent back to their homes in this country. He remembers *el barrio* Belvedere in East Los Angeles being emptied overnight. "They came at five in the morning with trucks and buses to drive them to Tijuana. Through a desire for vengeance and revenge, pachucos came from this experience." Pachucas were equals with their male peers because of equal victimization and codependency.

Most history books in this country are silent on this subject. To combat this vacuum of history, Stanford University Chicano students at Casa Zapata, the Chicano theme residence, annually celebrate Zoot Suit Month. For one month each year, talks, lectures, films, discussions, and workshops on the zoot suit, dress styles, hairdos, dancing, and music of that era are presented.

In a recent panel discussion entitled "El Pachuco: The Myth, the Legend, and the Reality," Fernando Soriano, a visiting psychology professor at Stanford, presented a study of contemporary Chicano gangs. He noted the lack of real role models for Chicano youth and how the figure of the pachuco fills the gap by offering a role model and a sense of rebellion against society, an opportunity to gain respect even if negative.

Professor Soriano noted the significant increases in gang activities and the growing number of Chicanas in gangs. From 452 gang-related homicides in 1988, the number jumped to 700 homicides in 1992 in LA. He questioned what gangs and homicides have to do with pachucos.

Fast to respond, José Montoya declared, "Gangs and homicides have nothing to do with pachucos. The drug lords dumped this shit on our barrios and we are stuck with it. The cartel brought in the drugs, firepower, and finances to move kids away from the fast food franchises." He went on to advise: "We need to lay down our fears about glamorizing the pachuco and showcase the important and viable aspects of the Chicano experience.

As offspring of Mexican and Mexican-American parents we need to see what it was like growing up. . . .

"Working-class servicemen from other parts of the country came thinking the LA barrios were exotic ports of entry. Seeing Chicanos for the first time freaked them out. Industrialists, such as newspaper mogul William Randolph Hearst, were already angry with Mexican president Cárdenas's nationalization of the oil industry. This wartime hysteria was translated for the Spanish language media, such as *La Opinión*. This didn't help Mexican and Mexican-American parents understand their children's rebellion."

Montoya calls the historical silence on these roundups shameful for this country, "but they shouldn't be for us. This is something that was put upon us at the same time Chicano soldiers were disproportionately winning more Congressional Medals of Honor than any other group. Pachucos were not all gangsters or *batos locos*. Some came from the fields and dressed up on weekends."

The third panel member, Renato Rosaldo, professor of social anthropology at Stanford and author of *Culture and Truth*, agreed with Montoya. Rosaldo noted the pachuco's exaggeration of the social norm: "putting it in your face. . . . The pachuco exaggeration is a way of producing cultural resistance, a cultural style to modify the existing norm with little or no Mexican symbolism. There is a kind of reverse resistance," he added, "the slow and low of a lowrider when the opposite American ethic is fast and efficient." Nothing is so infuriating as a car that's going very slow and low. Worse than speeding.

Rosaldo noted the dress styles and how the body goes beyond the clothes to become part of the style. Instead of leaning slightly forward, slouch shouldered like business men, the pachucos leaned back, shoulders thrown back and with long hand gestures. There is a Mexicanness in the formality along with self-dramatization and theatricality. Whereas the Anglo-American norm tends to be spontaneous, "be yourself," and informal, without spelling it out or being self-conscious.

In *American Me* Rosaldo saw very little heroism left in the heroic figure, finding instead a devastating criticism of a version of masculinity where there is no alternative. Olmos seemed to be crying out, "Stop the war! Wherever this stuff is coming from, it's destroying us!"

Rosaldo also believes it is demeaning to us to believe that a style of dress is responsible for the present-day tragedies. A good example is the zoot suit style of dress. The origin of the zoot suit has been traced to New York and Detroit, but it goes further back to Europe. In an interview conducted by Chuy Varela of Berkeley, California, renowned musician Cab Calloway traced the zoot suit to England. In the thirties, according to Calloway, the British clothing industry manufactured thousands of zoot suits as the latest style they thought would take hold. It didn't catch on and so they were dumped on the U.S. market. When they reached New York and Harlem in particular, African Americans took to them with pleasure and satisfaction. From New York's Harlem they were passed on to Detroit and Chicago. Those were the direct lines of migration for African Americans. For the Mexican-American urban migrants it was El Paso, Chicago, Detroit, and Los Angeles. African American ghettos, jobs, modest modes of transportation, music, and styles of dress greatly attracted Mexican Americans.

The comparisons between yesterday's pachucos and today's cholos are fascinating. Psychohistorian and USC professor Mauricio Mazón authored the book *The Zoot-Suit Riots: The Psychology of Symbolic Annihilation.* During and after the riots, Mexican-American youth were known to have shaved their heads, "a kind of scarification that indicated their victimization by servicemen." Fifty years later, some cholos tattoo a black tear below one of their eyes as a mark of incarceration.

Cholos are cultural descendants of the pachucos. A cholo is defined as a mestizo of Indian and European blood in most Spanish dictionaries. A secondary definition is tinged with Old World bigotry, identifying a cholo as a "civilized Indian." The term came to this country through the many Peruvians who arrived here during the California gold rush. It was used to describe Indians living along the Peruvian Coast. In California the Peruvians called poor mestizos "cholos."

Closely related to the word *cholo* is the term *bato*. Pancho Villa's revolutionary army was made of *batos vagos*, vagrant friends. *Batos vagos* has further evolved to the caló slang *batos locos*, crazy dudes. Caló, better known as Spanglish or Mex-Tex, has been utilized by the pachuco and the cholo both. Caló was originally *zincaló*, the idiom of Spanish gypsies. Interestingly enough, *calcos* is the same word pachucos, cholos, and gypsies use for shoes.

In Mexico, the pachuco was seen as the Anglo-Americanization of a Mexicano or, according to Paz, an extremity of what a Mexicano can become. In Mexico pachucos were called Tarzanes, perhaps because pachucos had long hair like Tarzan in the popular movies. Through Mexican comedian and film actor Germán Valdés, popularly known as Tin Tan, the pachuco became a novelty in Mexico.

Tin Tan has to be credited with taking Mexican-American influences to Mexico in the form of dress styles, music, caló, and English words. Valdés was the son of a Mexican consul who took his family to live in Laredo, El

Paso, and Los Angeles. When Tin Tan was young he befriended Mexican-American pachucos, took their music and style, and introduced it with humor on Mexico City stages and theater. He made over one hundred films and became a legend. In Juárez, Mexico, a zoot-suited Tin Tan sculpture looks over the old *mercado*.

The pachuco was also called a *tirilongo*, and though the word's origin is vague, pachucologist José Montoya believes it might have come from pachucos declaring their citizenship at the bridge. Instead of declaring "U.S. citizen," they blurted, "tirilongo." *Tirilón* also meant long threads, thus *tirilongo* was a blend of the English and Spanish. But a *tirilona* was not a pachuca; she was an informant.

Social anthropologist José Cuellar, alias musician Doctor Loco, further sees the pachuco as one of the precursors to multiculturalism, without the pachuco knowing what the word meant. In style, language, dress, but especially in music, the pachuco borrowed from the Anglo-American, the African American, the Mexicano, and the Caribbean to create a new and different kind of music. We now call it transculturalism.

In the end, the pachuco was the precursor of the Chicanos and the Chicano Movement. The pachucos were the first Mexican Americans to rebel against this county and their mother country, the first to stake their own universal identity and independence from both oppressive cultures, to mold their own, a renaissance hybrid of both.

Beyond the Zoot Suit Riots are the unmistakable spiritual cries of aesthetic expression through pachucos, cholos, zoot suiters, low riders, murals, language, cholos. Through Chicano theater, film, literature, and art, there is an assertion, a cultural and aesthetic identity, that today takes its place as part of the American experience.

Quetzalcoatl

*I*n San Jose, California, the city council approved a sculpture of Quetzalcoatl (pronounced ket-zal-ko-atl) by Mexican sculptor Robert Graham
for Cesar Chavez Park. From the beginning, protests erupted from various
segments of the community, including some Chicanos who felt the money
could have been spent on their community needs.

In November 1994, the sculpture was unveiled amid protests by right-
wing religious zealots who denounced Quetzalcoatl as an ancient bloodthirsty god. Following the unveiling, the media picked up the protests and
they became even more vile and vicious. Columnists and cartoonists had
a field day, calling it a mound of dog poo, coiled feces. A *San Jose Mercury*
editorial wallowed in displeasure and called it a lump, "squat sculpture,"
lamenting that it was not a soaring, graceful bronze sculpture shooting up
to heaven. The sculpture could not be appreciated from the sidewalk across
the street.

Had these journalists been more familiar with pre-Colombian art, had
they visited el Museo Antropológico de México, often called the most

beautiful anthropological museum in the world and home to thousands of pre-Colombian artifacts and sculptures, they would have found many "squat sculptures" and many "lumps."

Robert Graham's sculpture of Quetzalcoatl captured the massive and unmovable spirit of Mesoamerica. It is close to the earth, like its people; it is the color of the earth, not of white doves or soaring chrome spirals. Quetzalcoatl is the connection between earth and sky, the plumed serpent. Its representation was recognized even in our own bodies: the spinal column reaches from our tail end to our cerebrum, a reminder of our evolution as reptiles.

The sculpture brought one of this continent's greatest leaders to this country. Five hundred and two years after the Spaniards thought they had destroyed Quetzalcoatl, he joined his descendants in San Jose. Forgotten and dismissed were the hundreds of indigenous people that traveled from Mexico and throughout the Southwest to San Jose to celebrate and honor Quetzalcoatl. There aren't that many indigenous sculptures in city parks, but they are proud of this one, regardless of those who wanted soaring sculptures, something that would reflect Euro-American aesthetics.

The word *quetzalcoatl* is a metaphor of sight and sound. The quetzal is a rare bird with green feathers inhabiting the highlands of Chiapas and Guatemala. *Co* means snake, and *atl* means water.

Quetzalcoatl was the name of one of the greatest lords of all time. He was not a god but a human being, a lord, like Christ. He personified the forces of heaven, earth, and water, a holy trinity not unlike the Christian Father, Son, and Holy Ghost. Consider the image of Christ being baptized in the water and the Holy Ghost in the form of a dove above Him. The parallels to Christianity are many. Quetzalcoatl was associated with Tlaloc, the rain god. Christ was baptized in water by John the Baptist.

The concept of bird, snake, and water is also illustrated in Mexico's national symbol. An eagle devouring a snake atop a cactus in the middle of a lake symbolized the founding of Tenochtitlan by the Aztecs after migrating south from Aztlán. Birds and snakes have never coexisted peacefully, and one of the very few birds capable of killing a snake is a giant eagle. These two animals represented the strong forces of heaven, the earth and the water.

Quetzalcoatl is credited with founding and creating one of the greatest civilizations in the world. A seminal figure in the history of Teotihuacán, Tula, Yucatán, Oaxaca, and most other Mesoamerican nations, Quetzalcoatl was the principal lord of the Toltecas, Aztecas, Mayas, Quiches, Olmecas, and other Mesoamerican Indians.

However, Quetzalcoatl was also a victim of the Spanish invasion of Mexico that forced implementation of the Roman Catholic dogma. Since then, Quetzalcoatl has forever been unfairly maligned as an evil god who instituted human sacrifices. The truth: Quetzalcoatl was as gentle and life-giving as Jesus or Buddha. He has been called "the moral hero and liberator of ancient Mesoamerica." Human sacrifices were never offered to Quetzalcoatl. They were offered to a God called Huitzilopochtli. According to Carlos Fuentes, that liberty was the light of knowledge and education, a light so powerful that it became the basis of legitimacy for all.

Quetzalcoatl is credited with the creation of a calendar, a measure of time more precise than the Julian calendar, the cultivation of corn, agriculture, the ethics and philosophy of Mesoamerican culture.

Quetzalcoatl was at one time a real historical person, but as with most legends his attributes become many, varied, and obscure to the point that time turned him into a god or a myth. Through Mesoamerican history, there are many other Quetzalcoatls, priests who were given his name or who took it.

The complexity of Quetzalcoatl and the number of other Quetzalcoatl priests and myths could never fit into this short essay. Nonetheless, this is a brief attempt to begin to appreciate part of the fascinating and brilliant ancient Mesoamerican lord who gave so much to the world.

A religion and cult developed around Quetzalcoatl at the same time as the decline and disappearance of various religious centers and cities such as Teotihuacán around AD 750 and 900. Quetzalcoatl was represented by the bird that symbolized the heavens; the serpent that symbolized celestial water, cloud, or rain; a dissected shell containing the wind; as a divine spirit, as regeneration and birth, the totality of the universe, the four cardinal directions with the center.

It was at this time that Quetzalcoatl passed from not only the historical person but also as god of cyclical time and of rain as Tlaloc. Various priests took the name of Quetzalcoatl and some became semi-lords.

One of those was Quetzalcoatl, sometimes represented as the god of the wind, Ehécatl, and creator of the first man and woman of the fifth sun. According to one myth, Quetzalcoatl became intoxicated with his rival Tezcatlipoca and lost his chastity. For this, Quetzalcoatl was cast from the Garden of Lords. Quetzalcoatl then journeyed to the sea and set himself afire.

Quetzalcoatl has also been called the Morning Star, or "One Reed." After his flaming death he descended to Mictlan, the place of death, battled successfully against satanic forces, and returned with the bones of a man and a woman. He then stabbed himself with these bones and like Christ's death on the cross redeemed humanity from damnation.

As the planet Venus, Quetzalcoatl traveled daily to the other world in the West and then appeared every morning as the Morning Star in the East. It was Venus that inspired their calendar. Through observation and precise mathematical calculations it was noted that each cycle lasted 584 days.

Numerous representations of Quetzalcoatl on various pyramids and pre-Columbian artifacts from Teotihuacán in the high plateaus to Chichen Itzá in the southern lowlands of Yucatán give testimony to his past existence. According to Tolteca legend, history, and Western calculations, Ce Acatl Topilitzin, better know as Quetzalcoatl, was born in 947 BC. This priest-king of Tula, the holy city of the Toltecas, founded a religion that was to do away with human offerings. He replaced them with offerings of snails, birds, and butterflies. Quetzalcoatl was a great lawgiver, civilizer, creative in the arts and crafts, inventor of the calendar, or Book of Fate. He was a priest and a king. According to the writings in the Codex Chimalpopoca, devils constantly hounded him to kill and commit human sacrifices. He refused because he loved his Tolteca vassals. Eventually, Quetzalcoatl was banished from Tula by the "bloodthirsty worshippers of Tezcatlipoca." His regime was followed by a reign of terror, hunger, war, and pestilence in Mexico.

The complexity of Quetzalcoatl continues. He is seen as a ladder from heaven to earth with man at the center ("on the third day he arose from the dead and ascended into heaven"). Quetzalcoatl is said to have ascended to the planets to become part of the sun, the source of all life. As the sun, Quetzalcoatl became a male, impregnating Mother Earth, to bring forth a son. In the Vienna Codex, there is a naked Quetzalcoatl suspended in heaven and receiving gifts from the Dual Lord and Lady above all. Quetzalcoatl as a ladder has also been compared to Hindu philosophy in its seven powers of nature.

When Luis Valdez founded El Teatro Campesino, he authored a manifesto entitled *Pensamiento Serpentino: A Chicano Approach to the Theater of Reality*. This Mayan philosophy was a serpentine concept of embracing time, constant evolution, growth, and a future where a deep sense of continuity prevails. The serpent annually crawls out of its own dead skin. All living things evolve and change. Quetzalcoatl, the feathered serpent, unified the symbolic spirituality of the feathers with the earth serpent. All life is dynamic and in a state of constant motion, constant change, constant evolution. The mountain ranges, the valleys, the rivers, and the coastlines were serpentine, all changing forever but always keeping their integrity. Quetzalcoatl became a symbolic savior, not a nostalgic or romantic figure but real.

In defense of Quetzalcoatl, George L. Vásquez, a scholar of Latin American history and culture, stated: "Quetzalcoatl the legendary lord was a positive figure who embodied the sky and the rain which fell from it, as well as regeneration and the founding of the human race itself. The historical Quetzalcoatl was a leader who stressed social ethics and established a humanistic tradition which has lasted until today. He taught people how to sing, how to be good of heart."

One Who Knows Finds No Humor in Prejudice

*I*n a country that values freedom of expression more than any other right, we acknowledge that even racists have a right to voice their opinions.

I wanted to write about the different types of racism, and even inject light humor into this subject, but I can't. I know prejudice; I've experienced it. Sometimes I can smell it, feel it, and even know how to handle it—sometimes.

I remember a coworker back in Mineral Wells, Texas, I was ready to pounce on because of his remarks. He backed off, explaining. "We can't help it. We were raised to hate Meskins."

Back in California, one block away from my home, a middle-aged neighbor asked me, "Why don't you go back where you came from? You don't even belong here!" He didn't know we had bought a house a block away.

Racism is not confined to certain states or certain people. I've found it everywhere, but there are people who tell me, "You are better off in California," or, "It's more subtle in California."

Subtlety is a mask, and sometimes I would rather experience the overt racism than the covert. I would rather see the enemy and have the challenge than the subtle puzzle.

I would rather a waiter or waitress tell me they don't serve Mexicans or Chicanos, rather than not tell me anything and let me sit there wondering if it's prejudice or oversight. Overt racism has been outlawed, but not covert racism.

When I was going to high school in the late fifties, our football team would travel to small West Texas towns where they would refuse to serve the "Mexican boys." We would have to go to the kitchen. Of course, the whole team would walk out.

Four months ago, my family and I were passing through a small town in northwestern Arizona and stopped to eat. We still don't believe our one-hour wait in the restaurant was an oversight since everyone else around us was getting served. It was a long wait for my seventy-five-year-old father, two hungry children, and two impatient parents.

I can't handle racism the way I used to when I was single because of my two children. On Monday, March 16, 1981, I had an article in the *San Jose Mercury News* dealing with undocumented workers. I received a hate letter at my home address.

There was no return, which tells me the writers knew they were doing something very unethical, or they lacked courage.

There might have been a time when such letters would be disregarded as heavy pranks by crackpots. Today's climate does not permit the attitude. There is a resurgence of the Ku Klux Klan, Nazism, and the radical right. We know what crackpots have done to the world in our lifetime.

There are those who believe that I am more Mexican than American. Although my name is José and I sympathize with the undocumented worker, that does not mean I am Mexican and agree with Mexico's policies.

I served four and half years of active duty with the U.S. Air Force, three years in inactive reserves, two years with the Central Intelligence Agency, and four years with the U.S. Civil Service. You tell me.

Racism is ignorance; it is a social disease. I do not hate racists. But when I get hate letters delivered to my home, I fear for my family. I'll have to get an unlisted number, learn to live with fear, and keep writing. Some people will have to get used to seeing Hispanic names such as Sue Martinez's or mine. They are as common as the names of our towns: San Jose, San Francisco, Palo Alto . . .

For Whites Only

*I*can certainly empathize with Gary Pearl, the thirty-nine-year-old Louisville, Kentucky, man who has a mental problem—working with blacks.

According to the *New York Times*, the Kentucky Workers' Compensation Board has ordered the city to find a job for Gary with all-white coworkers because he has a fear of working with blacks. While the city is looking, Mr. Pearl has been granted a disability benefit of $231.47 until he returns to work.

Like many blacks and Hispanics, I know the kind of stress Gary Pearl has undergone. Being the only white in an all-black office can be as stressful as being the only black or Hispanic in an all-white office.

The Kentucky Workers' Compensation Board has also ordered Pearl to undergo therapy. There's a lot of blacks and Hispanics that could help him out, other than by showing him the door.

For instance, I would suggest he see the movie about Jackie Robinson's life. He was the first black player to enter major league baseball in 1947. The movie shows the racial harassment he received from his own team, the opposition, umpires, and the fans.

Then there was James Howard Meredith. How would you like to have been the only black attending the University of Mississippi in 1962? And not even getting paid for it or receiving student aid or a federal loan.

Many times I've found myself as the only non-Anglo in a job setting. It hasn't been exactly a rose garden but then nobody ever promised me one. I've learned to not only accept it, but work at it. In order to be successful I've had to do the job properly if not perfectly. Anything less puts you at an unequal disadvantage.

Then there's also a special way of conducting oneself in an all-white setting. You don't want to seem too ethnic because then they will not take you seriously or they will stereotype you. For this I use my best official English only. But there have been embarrassing moments when I "sleeped"—I mean "slipped." Sometimes "sit" becomes "seat" and "choose" becomes "shoes" or vice versa.

And you can't be too humorous because then you become their cute token mascot. One has to suppress one's humor to some degree and laugh at some of the great bland humor whites are known for.

There's no problem going out to lunch with an all-white crowd to a white restaurant. But going to a Mexican restaurant with an all-white crowd can be a real job. I have to translate, explain, and describe each item on the menu and tell some the difference between flautas and menudo or between a burrito and chimichanga.

Morning greetings at an all-white office can be very different from our "Buenos días." They can range from complete silence to "Well, good morning, Brad, and how are you this fine day?" Nothing like starting the day with a question.

Blacks and Hispanics are terrific switch-hitters. They can tangle with whites on their own turf or with their own in blackese or Hispanicese. Unfortunately most whites are not familiar with switch-hitting. Some of this switch-hitting commonly results in what we usually call schizophrenia, or a split personality.

My schizophrenia has been acting up lately. I have noticed that since Reagan became president I feel myself more alienated from my Anglo countrymen. According to my own psychoanalysis this was brought about by Reagan's war on poverty, undocumented aliens, and Central Americans, thus giving me an acute case of Anglophobia. But there are solutions to problems such as Gary's and mine.

Why not go back to where we began, because that's where we seem to be regressing anyway.

My friend Charlie has the ultimate solution. We can start with the bus transit systems. Each bus would have different sections: one for whites only, one for blacks only, Hispanics only, and "Others" only. These sections, of course, would be further divided into smoking and nonsmoking sections. However, there would be only one condition to this sectionalization (as opposed to segregation), that whites take their turn sitting at the back of the bus.

Chicano Art

A War That Was Never Won

The most impressive Chicano art exhibit of all time is touring and taking the country by storm. Named CARA, the Chicano Art Resistance and Affirmation exhibit initiated the tour in Los Angeles a year ago in September, traveled to Denver, Albuquerque, and San Francisco, and in September opens in Fresno before continuing through Tucson, Washington DC, the Bronx, and San Antonio.

For more than twenty-five years, Chicano art was considered outlaw art, but today it has reached the inner sanctum of spacious city museums and gallery halls. That it prevailed and developed for so long is testimony to its indomitable spirit and aesthetics. It was art with a mission, sometimes so powerful it seemed to self-destruct once the message was delivered. It was proud, colorful, passionate, sometimes humorous, but always alive. It had a vibrant home in the community. But now it is encased in a historical exhibition that makes it look static, almost out of place, but not quite, for it is art. The exhibit presents many questions.

One of the most obvious is on the future of Chicano art: "¿Ahora que?"—Now what? The art is exceptional and within its original context even better, but in museums and galleries it reminds me too much of where Chicano art has been and its present direction. Chicano art does have a future but seems nebulous, not cohesive, and individualized by mainstream acceptance. Discussion panels focused mostly on artists talking to each other rather than with the audience.

Besides the aforementioned reasons, Chicano art arrived to mainstream institutions for other reasons: It's part of the postmodernist period that ethnic art helped bring about; successful individual Chicano artists have made it happen; museums and galleries must show diversity to justify tax dollars; a craze or curiosity for multiculturalism, especially Hispanic, Latino, and Chicano art.

The Sunbelt is hot. Throughout the country, Chicano art symbols and icons (jalapeños, coyotes, cacti, and Guadalupe Virgins) have been transformed into campy artwork: pastel blankets, towels, and rugs. But the brilliant colors have been bleached and made culturally safe for mainstream consumption. In the CARA exhibit you can see the real thing, harmless like a tiger behind a cage. The black eagles and brilliant colors can't hurt you. They were brought in from the wild for your viewing pleasure and to serve history and diversity.

There are too many cliché pieces. Victor Martinez, Chicano poet, asks, "How many Zapatas, Frida Kahlos, and cholos must we see before we tire of them?" For Victor, the exhibit is a hard lesson.

A most important and critical part of any major historical art exhibit is a catalog. It is the most essential recorded legacy and reference text of information left by any exhibit. One year after it opened in Los Angeles there was still no catalog, a painful metaphor of our literacy and educational problems. Its absence reflects the organization, purpose, and future of a Chicano art.

More than ninety artists are represented from throughout the country. As in most group exhibits of this size, evenness is difficult to maintain. But some pieces were obviously exhibited only because the artists were also the organizers of the show or were closely associated, not because they were aesthetically or historically deserving. It was to be inclusive of art from 1965 to 1985, yet there are pieces that were done after '85 or seem out of place.

It was at least five years in planning. I attended the first regional San Francisco meeting. The disorganization, bickering, and lack of communication from the organizing committees were so disconcerting that I informed them I would not participate. My letter was never answered until last year when I received a rejection letter with returned slides for an exhibit I had boycotted and forgotten about. I remained on the outside with many other Chicano artists not included.

Attendance has been exceptional. This Chicano art exhibit is worthwhile. Some of the best art is by the least-known artists. Some artists have crossed into the mainstream, maintaining their politics and individual direction. But in this exhibition there is no unity, direction, and resolution.

Subtitled "A Celebration of Chicano Art," the exhibit is like a *celebracio* of a war that was never won. Can Chicano artists really afford to gather and celebrate like so many black eagles, disregarding the crises facing the United Farm Workers, cholos, and dropouts? On exhibit and in real life are those very problems and conflicts they painted.

It's in the Mail

*M*ás tortillas!" With his fat fingers, Chapo slid the plastic red basket across the counter and poured the last of his Perla beer into his glass as he masticated a mouthful of hot chile verde. He then blew his nose with a paper napkin, cleared the effect of the chile, wiped his sweating brow, put a paper napkin in his coat pocket, and grabbed another from the chrome holder.

Juanita, the waitress, a young thin woman with a fondness for heavy and perfumed makeup brought more tortillas in a green basket and set it down in front of Chapo's plate. She leaned over the counter to hear what Chapo was about to say.

"Juanita! Have you seen Chivo?" Chapo's eyes blinked from her soft cleavage to her green eyes.

Between the blaring norteño music vibrating, the laughter, and the clacking of billiard balls, Juanita was barely able to catch the name.

"Chivo?" She repeated the name, opened a thought with a smile, and shook her head from side to side. "No! no, no, no! I haven't seen that cabrón! But I heard he won ten thou' in the lotería."

Chapo raised his head, opened his eyes wide, and studied her green eyes for traces of dishonesty. He then continued to masticate slowly, swallowed, and asked, "¿Cuándo? ¿Cuándo?"

"¡No sé! ¡No sé! . . . last week sometime." She slapped her hip and walked away.

Chapo finished his chile verde in silence and without appetite. Then he lifted his short but hefty body from the stool and placed six bills on the counter. After shaking a toothpick out of a bottle, he bid farewell, "¡Ay, te watcho, Juanita!"

"You're too generous, Chapo!"

In the dying heat of a hot September afternoon Chapo waddled two blocks and then turned into his apartment building and the elevator.

Breathing with slight discomfort, Chapo fumbled with his keys and finally entered his one-bedroom apartment. Inside the stuffy unventilated apartment Chapo picked up the telephone from a coffee table and walked into his bedroom with the extension line dragging behind. He opened his bedroom window a couple of inches.

Softly lying on his bed, he doubled up the pillow to support his fat neck. Then he placed the telephone on his broad mountain chest. Chapo forced a burp as he began to flip through his little black book.

When he had found the number, he leaned the receiver on his fat cheek and began to push the numbers.

"Ha-low?" the other end answered.

"Chivo!"

"Hey, Chapo! Crazy Chapo!" With this Chivo began his bleating laugh, just like a goat. It grated on Chapo's nerves.

"Crazy Chapo! He-he-he-he-he-he-! ¿Qué pasa, ese?"

Chapo didn't answer.

Chivo picked up on the silence. "Hey, Chapo, I'm painting again man! I'm actually painting again, man. I, ah, sold . . . ten paintings to the *American Scientific* magazine, Chapo, ahem." He cleared his throat again. "I'm going to send them to you, Chapo."

"What the hell for? I thought you sold them."

"Awww, c'mon, Chapo! Sell'em, Chapo! I sold three to the *American Scientific*. I'll send you the other seven!" Again, Chivo cleared his throat.

"I'm not a salesman, Chivo. What the hell do I want with your paintings?"

Chivo's feelings were bruised and Chapo knew it.

"¿De qué son, Chivo?"

"Huh?"

"What are they of, Chivo?"

"Ahh, bone structure . . . bone structure of the roadrunner, the *Geococyx texicanus*." With this Chivo cleared his throat once more.

"I don't want them, Chivo; I'm not going to sell them. That's not the way I collect."

"Hey, hey, Chapo! I'll send them to you. Do whatever you want with them and I'll send you a check for a hundred bucks."

"How much?" Chapo couldn't believe the amount he was hearing.

"The drawings and a check for two hundred dollars, Chapo."

Chapo laughed.

"Hey, c'mon, Chapo. Look!" Chivo cleared his throat and then whispered. "I lost my ass in a coke deal, Chapo. I was out of a job for a while there. I'm barely getting back on my feet . . . It's a bitch, Chapo."

"You've been drinking, Chivo."

"Me?" Chivo bleated his nervous laugh. "I drink all the time, Chapo." Chivo thought his answer hilarious and began to laugh more and louder. It irritated Chapo and so he removed the phone from his ear as he stared at the ceiling.

"How's la familia, Chivo?"

"Hey, all right. Fine! Jessie's eating us out of the house. We gotta horse living with us." Chivo again laughed expecting Chapo to also laugh.

"I've been waiting for a long time . . ." Chapo interrupted.

"As soon as I get paid for these drawings . . ."

"I've been waiting a long pinchi time, Chivo. I want my money back. I'm gonna have to send someone to collect for me. You're bad business for me, Chivo."

Chivo began to pace nervously as far as the extension cord would allow. "Wait, espera . . . give me time, Chapo. One pinchi week! What's today? Thursday! No! I mean Wednesday . . . Till next Thursday, Chapo. I'll have it in the pinchi mail, Chapo. Promise! If I don't, you can send someone." Chivo made a sign of the cross with his left thumb and forefinger and kissed it in front of the telephone receiver.

"Oye, Chivo! You know what the two biggest lies in the world are?"

"Huh?"

"'Brown is beautiful' and 'It's in the mail.' You ain't beautiful, you ain't even brown, and I don't trust the mail."

Chivo faked his bleating laughter, "Awww, c'mon, Chapo. Hey, buddy. Wait . . . wait . . . Here . . . talk to my wife." Chivo walked over to his wife and shoved the outstretched telephone into her ear. "Hon, Hon, talk to Chapo. Hon, tell'em we'll have the money in a week."

"Señor Chapo, ¿cómo está usted, señor Chapo? My husband—he gonna get it together, Meester Chapo. I gonna see he does it, okay? Bye!"

"Sí señora, seguro, by all means. If I have your word . . ."

Chivo took over the phone, "Thanks Chapo, you're very under . . ."

Click! Chapo flushed red with anger and heartburn as he hung up. He hated Chivo even more for putting his wife on the line. He looked through his telephone book again, marked another number, and waited.

"Mestas! Chapo here . . . no! . . . Gotta pencil? Here's the address, 2367 Eighth Street, corner of Ocho y Ochoa, Apartment 3. One kid . . . He doesn't want to share his good fortune. Can you beat that? I want you to do it today . . . Good. Let me know." Chapo hung up and put the phone down on the floor. He felt the acid burn his chest, and so he closed his eyes to relax.

Chivo let out a bleating laugh as he turned to his wife. "Chapo will be surprised when he gets his mail tomorrow. I made him sweat for it." He laughed again and asked his wife, "You did mail it, didn't you?"

La Puerta

*I*t had rained in thundering sheets every afternoon that summer. A dog-tired Sinesio returned home from his job in a mattress sweatshop. With a weary step from the autobús, Sinesio gathered the last of his strength and darted across the busy avenida into the ramshackle colonia where children played in the meandering pathways that would soon turn into a noisy arroyo of rushing water. The raindrops striking the barrio's tin, wooden, and cardboard roofs would soon become a sheet of water from heaven.

Every afternoon Sinesio's muffled knock on their two-room shack was answered by Faustina, his wife. She would unlatch the door and return to iron more shirts and dresses of people who could afford the luxury. When thunder clapped, a frightened Faustina would quickly pull the electric cord, believing it would attract lightning. Then she would occupy herself with preparing dinner. Their children would not arrive home for another hour.

On this day Sinesio laid down his tattered lunch bag, a lottery ticket, and his week's wages on the oily tablecloth. Faustina threw a glance at the lottery ticket.

Sinesio's silent arrival always angered Faustina, so she glared back at the lottery ticket. "Throwing money away! Buying paper dreams! We can't afford dreams, and you buy them."

Sinesio ignored her anger. From the table he picked up a letter, smelled it, studied the U.S. stamp, and with the emphatic opening of the envelope sat down at the table and slowly read aloud the letter from his brother Aurelio as the rain beat against the half-tin, half-wooden rooftop.

Dear Sinesio,

I write to you from this country of abundance, the first letter I write from los Estados Unidos. After two weeks of nerves and frustration I finally have a job at a canning factory. It took me that long only because I did not have the necessary social security number. It's amazing how much money one can make but just as amazing how fast it goes. I had to pay for the social security number, two weeks of rent, food, and a pair of shoes. The good pair you gave me wore out on our journey across the border. From the border we crossed two mountains, and the desert in between.

I will get ahead because I'm a better worker than the rest of my countrymen. I can see that already and so does the "boss." Coming here will be hard for you, leaving Faustina and the children. It was hard enough for me and I'm single without a worry in life. But at least you will have me here if you come and I'm sure I can get you a job. All you've heard about the crossing is true. Even the lies are true. "Saludos" from your "compadres" Silvio and Ramiro. They are doing fine. They're already bothering me for the bet you made against the Dodgers.

Next time we get together I will relate my adventures and those of my compañeros . . . things to laugh and cry about.

Aurelio signed the letter *Saludos y abrazo*. Sinesio looked off into space and imagined himself there already. But this dreaming was interrupted by the pelting rain and Faustina's knife dicing nopal, cactus, on the wooden board.

"¿Qué crees?"—What do you think? Faustina asked Sinesio.

"¡No sé!"—I don't know, Sinesio responded with annoyance.

"But you do know, Sinesio. How could you not know? There's no choice. We have turned this over and around a thousand times. That miserable mattress factory will never pay you enough to eat with. We can't even afford the mattresses you make."

Sinesio's heart sank as if he was being pushed out or had already left his home. She would join her comadres as another undocumented widow.

Already he missed his three children, Celso, Jenaro, and Natasia his eldest, a joy every time he saw her. "An absence in the heart is an empty pain," he thought.

Faustina reminded Sinesio of the inevitable trip with subtle statements and proverbs that went straight to the heart of the matter. "Necessity knows no frontiers," she would say. The dicing of nopal and onions took on the fast clip of the rain. Faustina looked up to momentarily study a trickle of water that had begun to run on the inside of a heavily patched glass on the door. It bothered her, but unable to fix it at the moment, she went back to her cooking.

Sinesio accepted the answer to a question he wished he had never asked. The decision was made. There was no turning back. "I will leave for el norte in two weeks," he said gruffly and with authority.

Faustina's heart sank as she continued to make dinner. After the rain, Sinesio went out to help his compadre widen a ditch to keep the water from flooding in front of his door. The children came home, and it became Faustina's job to inform them that Papá would have to leave for a while. None of them said anything. Jenaro refused to eat. They had expected and accepted the news. From their friends, they knew exactly what it meant. Many of their friends' fathers had already left and many more would follow.

Throughout the following days, Sinesio continued the same drudgery at work, but as his departure date approached he began to miss even that. He secured his family and home, made all the essential house repairs he had put off, and asked his creditors for patience and trust. He asked his sisters, cousins, and neighbors to check on his family. Another compadre lent him money for the trip and the coyote. Sinesio did not know when he would return, but told everyone, "One year, no more. Save enough money, buy things to sell here and open up a negocio, a small business the family can help with."

The last trip home from work was no different except for the going-away gift, a bottle of mezcal, and the promise of his job when he returned. As usual, the autobús was packed. And as usual, the only ones to talk were two loud young men, sinvergüenzas—without shame.

The two young men talked about the Lotería Nacional and a lottery prize that had gone unclaimed for a week. "¡Cien millones de pesos!—One hundred million pesos! ¡Carajo!" one of them kept repeating as he slapped the folded newspaper on his knees again and again. "Maybe the fool that bought it doesn't even know!"

"Or can't read!" answered the other. And they laughed with open mouths.

This caught Sinesio's attention. Two weeks earlier he had bought a lottery ticket. "Could . . .? No!" he thought. But he felt a slight flush of blood rush to his face. Maybe this was his lucky day. The one day out of thousands that he had lived in poverty.

The two jumped off the bus, and Sinesio reached for the newspaper they had left behind. There on the front page was the winning number. At the end of the article was the deadline to claim the prize—8:00 that night.

Sinesio did not have the faintest idea if his ticket matched the winning number. So he swung from the highest of hopes and dreams to resigned despair as he wondered if he had won one hundred million pesos.

Jumping off the bus, he ran home, at times slowing to a walk to catch his breath. The times he jogged, his heart pounded, the newspaper clutched in his hand, the heavy gray clouds ready to pour down.

Faustina heard his desperate knock and swung the door open.

"¿Dónde está?" Sinesio pleaded. "Where is the lottery ticket I bought?" He said it slowly and clearly so he wouldn't have to repeat himself.

Faustina was confused. "What lottery ticket?"

Sinesio searched the table, under the green, oily cloth, on top of the dresser, and through his papers, all the while with the jabbing question: "What did you do with the boleto de lotería?"

Thunder clapped. Faustina quit searching and unplugged the iron. Sinesio sounded off about no one respecting his papers and how no one could find anything in that house. "¿Dónde está el boleto de lotería?"—Where is the lottery ticket?

They both stopped to think. The rain splashed into a downpour against the door. Faustina looked at the door to see if she had fixed the hole in the glass.

"¡La puerta!"—The door! blurted Faustina. "I put in on the door to keep the rain from coming in."

Sinesio turned to see the ticket glued on the broken window pane. It was light blue with red numbers and the letters *Lotería Nacional*. Sinesio brought the newspaper up to the glued lottery ticket and with his wife compared the numbers one by one: "Seis – tres – cuatro – uno – ocho –nueve – uno – ¡SIETE – DOS!"—Sinesio yelled.

"¡No!" trembled a disbelieving and frightened Sinesio. "One hundred million pesos!" His heart pounded, afraid this was all a mistake, a bad joke. They checked it again and again only to confirm the matching numbers.

Sinesio then tried to peel the ticket off. His fingernail slid off the cold, glued lottery ticket. Faustina looked at Sinesio's stubby fingernails and moved in. But Faustina's thinner fingernails also slid off the lottery ticket.

Sinesio walked around the kitchen table looking, thinking, trying to remain calm.

Then he grew frustrated and angry. "What time is it?"

"A quarter to seven," Faustina said, looking at the alarm clock above the dresser. They tried hot water and a razor blade with no success. Sinesio then lashed out at Faustina in anger. "You! I never answered your mockery! Your lack of faith in me! I played the lottery because I knew this day would come! ¡Por Dios Santo!" and he swore and kissed his crossed thumb and forefinger. "And now? Look what you have done to me, to us, to your children!"

"We can get something at the farmacia! The doctor would surely have something to unglue the ticket!"

"¡Sí! ¡O sí!" mocked Sinesio. "Sure! We have time to go there."

Time runs faster when there is a deadline. The last bus downtown was due in a few minutes. They tried to take the broken glass pane off the door, but Sinesio was afraid the ticket would tear more. His fear and anger mounted with each glance at the clock.

In frustration, he pushed the door out into the downpour and swung it back into the house, cracking the molding and the inside hinges. One more swing, pulling, twisting, splintering, and Sinesio broke the door completely off.

Faustina stood back with hands over her mouth as she recited a litany to all the santos and virgins in heaven as the rain blew into their home and splashed her face wet.

Sinesio's face was also drenched. But Faustina could not tell if it was from the rain or tears of anger, as he put the door over his head and ran down the streaming pathway to catch the autobús.

Redwood City

In Redwood City
people awoke one day
      to screaming hieroglyphics
         no one could decipher
            but the cholos.

Overnight, Madera Roja
became worthwhile
for squad cars
      and políticos
         to practice their tactics
            while the cowboy bar disappeared.

In Madera Roja
along Middlefield Road,
viejos from Michoacán,
walk up and down
yearning for a softer ground

and tipping their hats
       to señoras in mourning black.

In El Bracero Bar,
       Los Inocentes
              play old norteñas
              on electric guitars
                     while young men
                     sip Coors
                     glancing at the prancing güeras,
                            wishing . . .
                     In Madera Roja
                     la tierra de México
                            has been traded for dust.

In Madera Roja,
young *cholos* and *cholas*
guard the street corners
       and stake their claim
              for the long wait.

El Juan from Sanjo

El Juan from Sanjo
    whispers cobwebs
    into the telephone
        as if he were still in Soledad
            knitting compromises
                between the bars of his life
                    and with melancholic care
                    he whispers:

Sabes que, ese?
I'm a loco from the word go,
    in the purest sense
        of the word *loco*,
        from the latin,
            loco citato,
                the place cited,
            I know my place, ese,
                I know my location,

my station
¡es aquí!
¿Entiendes mendez?

El Juan
    speaks his thoughts
        between blowouts
            and consultations
            with Kierkegaard:
            "¡Me explota la mente, ese!"

On the relevance
of graffiti on the wall:
    "They wash it off or paint it out.
        That's the crux of the problem, ese!
            The people don't read!"

Sister María de la Natividad
Burciaga Zapata

26th of Angst
     nineteen–eighty something
         11:30 stranded desert time.

Today tía Nati,
my brown indian aunt
     in a black habit
     passed away.

She who baptized my entrance
and performed bendiciones
     on my scarred face
         with a white smile
           and a letanía
              de los santos
                    now and at the
                    hour of my wake.

Unlike other nuns,

tía Nati died beneath a bed
    speaking in tongues
        and celebrating freedom
        from her sanity.

It all began and ended as a dream
    the day she was born.

Today she rests
alive in the reality
    of an eternity
        more real
        than this fleeting space
            called time.

PART FOUR: *Virgin Variations*

Editor's note: La Virgen María is one of the most important cultural-political-spiritual images of Mexican and Chicano culture. Obviously a presence that is so important will find its way into Chicano/a art. Chicano/a artists and writers have not only accepted her as a source of artistic inspiration but have redefined her in empowering ways. Just as the United Farm Workers used her image at political rallies, strikes, and marches, Chicano/a artists have used her image to assert everything from a specific political-cultural issue to the empowerment of women. The editors of this book were excited to have found an unpublished, never-before-seen artist's pad in which Burciaga drew variations of la Virgen de Guadalupe. We copied these images directly from the pad. What follows is an exciting discovery from a great artist. Notice the different cultural manifestations of la Virgen, from indigenous to urban Chicana to la Lucha Libre, the masked ring fighters popular in Mexico. Many of these drawings are humorous without being irreverent. All of them together express the omnipresence of la Virgen María in the lives of her Mexican-Chicano children. We are proud to present these virgin variations for first time.

25 DE ε 92

Virgin. Not seen before by the public, all these images are from a sketch pad. All are of la Virgen de Guadalupe, many of them humorous or satirical, yet all of them reverent toward the Holy Mother, the protector of Mexico and of the Chicano Movement. This first image is perhaps the most conventional rendering in the bunch.

Virgin 2. Notice how the aura around the Virgin seems to becoming more like feathers, perhaps relating her spiritually to Mexico's indigenous, whose goddess, Tonantzin, is believed by many to be another manifestation of la Virgencita.

Picasso Virgin. This image evokes a bit of cubism or postmodern uses of perspective. Notice the handbag that la Virgencita carries and the low-cut dress, a modern woman to go with this modern rendering.

Native Virgin. This image makes the Virgin a Native American, with feathers and moccasins. Although she has traditionally been thought of as indigenous and is often called la Morenita (the little brown one), in this image she could be native to North America.

17.4.93

Native Virgin. Here she becomes even more Native American. Notice the
bull's head that supports her weight, a shift from the angel that carries her in
the more traditional images.

Indigenous Virgin. Here she is shortened and given a round face, perhaps identifying her with other indigenous peoples of Mexico. The aura around her has gone from feathers in the preceding images to perhaps corn leaves in this rendering.

Virgin of the Night. This is a kind of sophisticated, big-city image of the
Virgin. Notice that the angel who supports her wears a headband, a bandana,
like a cool Chicano from East LA.

Lucha Libre Virgin. The Virgin becomes a *luchadora,* a fighter in Mexico's *Lucha Libre,* which is very popular among the common people. This image seems to say that the Virgin is also with the people. The aura around her has become lightning bolts of power.

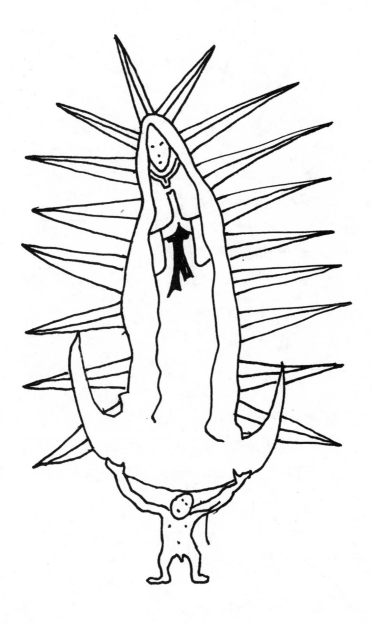

Lifting the Virgin. Here the angel lifting the Virgin is most like a luchador. The aura now becomes like the leaves of the maguey plant, native to Mexico, from which tequila is made.

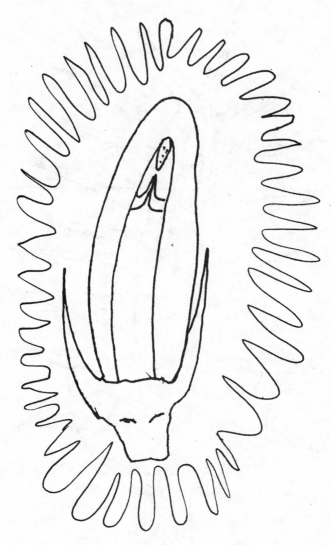

17·4·93

Texas Virgin. This seems to have a Texas flair, the longhorn bull replacing the angel that lifts the Virgin to glory.

Chola Virgin. Here la Virgencita become like a *cholita*, la Lupe, like a tough girl from the barrio. She is an urban Chicana, a *loca*. The teardrop may evoke the tattoo teardrop sported by Chicanos who have been to prison, indicating *la vida loca*, the crazy street life.

Jesus Virgin. Here she becomes the image of Christ. In many parts of Mexico and among many people, La Virgin is as important a savior as the son she bore.

PART FIVE: *Cooks and Comidas*

Panza llena, corazón contento.
Full belly, happy heart.

Migajas también son pan y buen alimento dan.
Crumbs are bread too, and will also nourish you.

Contigo, pan y cebolla.
With you, bread and onions.
(I'll stick by you through thick and thin.)

Llamar al pan, pan y al vino, vino.
Call bread bread, and wine wine.
(Call it as you see it.)

En mesa ajena, la tripa llena.
On another's bill, eat your fill.

A la boca amarga, la miel le sabe a retama.
To a bitter mouth, honey tastes sour.

A Bohemian's Toast

*G*uillermo Aguirre y Fierro was not a well-known Mexican poet when he entered an obscure cantina in a south El Paso barrio and sat down to write a poem. That was more than sixty years ago.

The poem he wrote, "El Brindis del Bohemio" (A Bohemian's Toast), is better known today than his name. It is recited the Spanish-speaking world over, from Mexico to Spain, Argentina, and this country. Within many extended families, there is always someone who can recite it at family gatherings on New Year's Eve.

Aguirre y Fierro wrote of six happy bohemians celebrating the last hours of a New Year's Eve. Among the bottles of rum, whiskey, and Scotch there was drinking and laughter that continuously curled and dissipated with the cigarette smoke into the quiet barrio night. With each drink they found themselves further away from the pain and suffering of the passing year. The clock struck twelve and there were shouts of joy welcoming the Feliz Año Nuevo.

A voice spoke up. "It's twelve, *compañeros*. Let us leave the year that now becomes a part of the past. Let us drink to this year that begins. May it bring us dreams and not the baggage of bitter sorrows."

Another voice arose. "I toast for the hope that launches us into life to conquer the rigors of destiny. For hope, our sweet friend, that softens our pains and converts our path into a flower garden . . ." He toasted hope, a star that had enlightened him after a bitter love affair. "Bravo!" Everyone loved the toast. "You're inspired tonight. You've said it well; briefly and with substance."

It was Raúl's turn. He raised his cup and toasted to Europe. "Her delicious exoticism . . . I drink and toast to my past life, one of light, love, and joy in which tempting women found my dreams." Raúl continued: "I toast for the yesterdays that today console my bitterness and sad soul. My memory transcends to the sweet joys of tenderness, love, and delightful sleepless nights."

"I toast," said Juan, "because I am overcome with inspiration, divine and seductive, because within the cords of my life lives the verse that sighs, smiles, sings, loves, and is loved . . ." His beautiful toast continued, but soon turned bitter, remembering an ungrateful woman with a beautiful body but a heart of granite. He hoped that with his song he could reach her heart and passion. "I toast that I may get inebriated on the divine nectar of her kisses."

The tempest of vain and coarse verses continued. They toasted the nation, the chaste loves that were soon violated, and the voluptuous passions that make one blush and convert the woman into a courtesan.

Only one toast was left, that of Arturo, the bohemian of a pure, noble heart and great intelligence. It was Arturo, whose only declared desire was to steal inspiration from sadness. He stood up, raised his cup, and, before an overbearing crowd noisy with laughter and joy, embraced them with the penetrating light of his gaze. He shook his long hair and with an inspired tone declared: "I toast to womanhood, but not to that one in which you find comfort . . . and cinders of pleasure.

"I do not toast to her, *compañeros*. I feel this time I cannot please you. I toast to the woman who embraced me with her kisses, to the woman who rocked my cradle, to the woman who taught me as a child the value of exquisite love, profound and real, to the woman who lulled me in her arms and gave me in pieces, one by one, her entire heart.

"To my mother, bohemians! To the old woman who thinks of tomorrow as something sweet and desired, because perhaps she dreams destiny will show me the path and I will soon return close to her side.

"To the old woman, loved and blessed. To the one who with her blood gave me life, tenderness, and love. To the one who became the light of my soul. To her I toast; let me cry these flowers of tears, this pain that kills me. To the sad, old woman who suffers and cries, and to the heavens implores that I return to be with her.

"To my mother, bohemians, who is melted sweetness and the star in the bitterness of my black nights."

Arturo, the bohemian, stopped. No one dared desecrate that pronouncement born of love and tenderness that floated over the atmosphere like an immense poem of love.

Of Guillermo Aguirre y Fierro not much is known, but his poem lives and is recited each New Year's Eve wherever Spanish-speaking mothers live.

¡Feliz Año Nuevo!

I Remember Masa

My earliest memory of tortillas is my mamá telling me not to play with them. I had bitten eyeholes in one and was wearing it as a mask at the dinner table.

As a child, I also used tortillas as hand warmers on cold days, and my family claims that I owe my career as an artist to my early experiments with tortillas. According to them, my clowning around helped me develop a strong artistic foundation. I'm not so sure, though. Sometimes I wore a tortilla on my head, like a yarmulke, and yet I never had any great urge to convert from Catholicism to Judaism. But who knows? They may be right.

For Mexicans over the centuries, the tortilla has served as the spoon and the fork, the plate and the napkin. Tortillas originated before the Mayan civilizations, perhaps predating Europe's wheat bread. According to Mayan mythology, the great god Quetzalcoatl, realizing that the red ants knew the secret of using maize as food, transformed himself into a black ant, infiltrated the colony of red ants, and absconded with a grain of corn. (Is it any wonder that to this day, black ants and red ants do not get along?)

Quetzalcoatl then put maize on the lips of the first man and woman, Oxomoco and Cipactonal, so that they would become strong. Maize festivals are still celebrated by many Indian cultures of the Americas.

When I was growing up in El Paso, tortillas were part of my daily life. I used to visit a tortilla factory in an ancient adobe building near the open *mercado* in Ciudad Juárez. As I approached, I could hear the rhythmic slapping of the *masa* as the skilled vendors outside the factory formed it into balls and patted them into perfectly round corn cakes between the palms of their hands. The wonderful aroma and the speed with which the women counted so many dozens of tortillas out of warm wicker baskets still linger in my mind. Watching them at work convinced me that the most handsome and *deliciosas* tortillas are handmade. Although machines are faster, they can never adequately replace generation-to-generation experience. There's no place in the factory assembly line for the tender slaps that give each tortilla character. The best thing that can be said about mass-producing tortillas is that it makes it possible for many people to enjoy them.

In the mercado where my mother shopped, we frequently bought *taquitos de nopalitos*, small tacos filled with diced cactus, onions, tomatoes, and jalapeños. Our friend don Toribio showed us how to make delicious, crunchy taquitos with dried, salted pumpkin seeds. When you had no money for the filling, a poor man's taco could be made by placing a warm tortilla on the left palm, applying a sprinkle of salt, then rolling the tortilla up quickly with the fingertips of the right hand. My own kids put peanut butter and jelly on tortillas, which I think is truly bicultural. And speaking of fast foods for kids, nothing beats a quesadilla, a tortilla grilled-cheese sandwich.

Depending on what you intend to use them for, tortillas may be made in various ways. Even a run-of-the-mill tortilla is more than a flat corn cake. A skillfully cooked homemade tortilla has a bottom and a top; the top skin forms a pocket in which you put the filling that folds your tortilla into a taco. Paper-thin tortillas are used specifically for flautas, a type of taco that is filled, rolled, and then fried until crisp. The name *flauta* means "flute," which probably refers to the Mayan bamboo flute; however, the only sound that comes from an edible flauta is a delicious crunch that is music to the palate. In México flautas are sometimes made as long as two feet and then cut into manageable segments. The opposite of flautas is gorditas, meaning "little fat ones." These are very thick small tortillas.

The versatility of tortillas and corn does not end here. Besides being tasty and nourishing, they have spiritual and artistic qualities as well. The

Tarahumara Indians of Chihuahua, for example, concocted a corn-based beer called *tesgüino*, which their descendants still make today. And everyone has read about the woman in New Mexico who was cooking her husband a tortilla one morning when the image of Jesus Christ miraculously appeared on it. Before they knew what was happening, the man's breakfast had become a local shrine.

Then there is tortilla art. Various Chicano artists throughout the Southwest have, when short of materials or just in a whimsical mood, used a dry tortilla as a small, round canvas. And a few years back, at the height of the Chicano Movement, a priest in Arizona got into trouble with the church after he was discovered celebrating mass using a tortilla as a host. All of which only goes to show that while the tortilla may be a lowly corn cake, when the necessity arises, it can reach unexpected distinction.

Pressing Issues

There are many kinds of corn, many colors, and many sizes, ranging from those tiny, cute canned ears of corn to the Texas-size twelve-inchers. The most common type for making tortillas is white corn, with a big, meaty kernel, but your choice of colors does not stop here. Blue tortillas are one of the Southwest's finest products. Made from a natural variety of Indian blue corn, these tortillas have a deep slate blue cast. There is also red and even black corn. I have always felt that red, white, and blue tortillas would be a great Fourth of July food, but I fear that the Daughters of the American Revolution would frown on the idea.

Like in everything else, there are good, bad, and indifferent tortillas. A connoisseur can smell the quality of superior tortillas, and the only way to become a connoisseur is to learn the ins and outs of making them yourself.

You begin your lesson by buying the freshly prepared masa from a tortilla factory. If you live anywhere in the Southwest, there is probably one close to you. Just look in the Yellow Pages. The only time when it may be difficult to get the masa is around Christmas, when everyone is making tamales for Christmas Eve and New Year's Eve. But even so, it's not a bad idea to call first, because tortillas are made early in the morning and delivered throughout the day, and the factory might run short of masa. You can also use Quaker instant *masa harina*, which is carried by most supermarkets. The instructions are on the package. But don't try to use cornmeal; it will not do at all.

Now, let's say you ran out to your local tortilla factory and bought one and a half pounds of prepared masa. While you were in the store you noticed several objects that looked like small printing presses. You asked what they were and the man told you they were tortilla presses. You blushed at your ignorance and decided you'd better get one. And it is best, unless you plan to slap the masa from one hand to the other till you get a perfectly round tortilla, which may very well be never. Take it from me, you are better off with a tortilla press, and the sturdier and heavier the better. They usually cost seven to ten dollars.

To be as authentic as possible you should also have a *comal*. What is a comal? A comal is a round, flat, iron griddle that you put over the burner. They are hard to come by in the United States, but fortunately you can get by without one. One or two big heavy metal pans, lightly greased, will do nicely. An electric griddle will do in a pinch, but sometimes it does not give sufficient heat.

You are now almost ready to make the first of many tortillas in your lifetime. The last things you need are two pieces of waxed paper or, better still, two pieces of polyethylene from a sandwich bag. Ideally, the plastic should be from a Bimbo Mexican brand bread wrapper. Put one of these pieces on the bottom plate of the press, roll a ball of masa one to two inches in diameter, and then set it down lightly on the plastic. Put the second piece of plastic on top of the dough ball and squeeze the top of the press down very firmly. Open it and peel off the top piece of plastic, then place the tortilla in your hand and peel off the other piece of plastic. The order is important. If you try to peel the tortilla off the plastic, I guarantee you will make a big mess and have to start over.

Before you cook your creation, take one last look at it. Is it too *gorda*? You didn't press hard enough. Is it too grainy or too *seca*? Well, amigo, you can still put a little more water in the dough, but don't add too much or you will have another fine mess and the plastic will never come off your tortilla. When you're sure all is going well, carefully lay the tortilla on a hot pan or griddle over medium heat. Some people like to slam them down and watch air bubbles form in the dough, but that results in a tortilla with a somewhat cratered surface.

You are anxiously watching your first tortilla cook on the griddle. When you see that the edges have begun to dry, flip it over; if you let the edges dry out completely, they will be hard. How do you flip it? Unless you have quick, experienced fingers, you'd better use a spatula. After cooking the tortilla on the second side, flip it back to the first side. If the masa and the heat are just right, the tortilla will now puff up. The side that puffs up is the right side, the thin top skin; this forms the fold pocket where the fillings go when you make tacos.

When your tortilla is done, pick it up from the griddle and place it between the folds of a thick kitchen towel or in a wicker tortilla basket with a sombrero top, which you get at an import store. These baskets insulate very effectively. Just put a cloth napkin inside to absorb condensation. Continue pressing and cook one tortilla at a time until the basket is full. Don't press all the tortillas at once, or they will dry out.

Now, all this may seem a little trying the first time around, but before you know it, making tortillas will become second nature. You can easily reheat them by wrapping them in foil and setting them in a 300-degree oven or toaster oven for five minutes. And one of the best and highest uses of the microwave oven is reheating tortillas; you can do a dozen in less than three minutes, and they will stay moist.

Another method we sometimes use at home is to heat a pan and use it like a comal. But by far the best way to warm a tortilla is to lay it directly over the flames of a gas burner for a few seconds. I have amazed many a gringo friend by sticking my fingers into the fire to flip a tortilla. An electric burner will work too, but you'll have to experiment to find the right setting. If the heat is too intense, in one second your tortilla will burn and taste awful. There are many ways to reheat tortillas, and it doesn't matter which one you use as long as you don't let them go to waste.

Flour Power

The flour tortilla, *comadre* to the corn tortilla, has a much shorter history. The flour tortilla originated in the state of Sonora, the breadbasket of México. Like its maize counterpart, the flour *tortilla de harina* has many forms, sizes, and styles. It is common in northern México and in the southwestern United States but not at all well known around Mexico City.

In South Texas flour tortillas are small and thick. In West Texas they are medium sized. In California it's a mixture, though big, thin types predominate. In Sonora and adjacent Arizona, tortillas de harina are large, eighteen to twenty-four inches in diameter. There they are folded and put next to your plate like napkins. The last time I was in Phoenix, instead of asking for a doggie bag I asked for an extra tortilla to carry the leftovers in. Later that night I had a fantastic burrito for a snack.

When a burrito is fried and served with guacamole and salsa on top, it becomes a chimichanga.

Flour tortillas spoil faster than corn tortillas, though they do make wonderful sandwiches, even at classroom temperature. I remember going to school with a *burrito de chorizo con huevo* (Mexican sausage and eggs) and staining my brown lunch bag and khaki pants with grease. Across the schoolyard sat my friend Suzy with her Roy Rogers lunchbox, spilling peanut butter and jelly from her white-bread sandwich onto her freshly pressed dress. For kids, cultural differences are sometimes not so large after all.

To make two dozen flour tortillas you need:

1 pound of sifted white flour
2 teaspoons salt
¼ cup of lard
1 cup of warm water

Place the flour into a bowl and cut in the lard as if you were making piecrust. Dissolve the salt in the water and add to the flour and lard to make a pliable dough; knead it until it is soft and elastic. Grease your hands and form dough balls one and a half inches in diameter or slightly bigger. On a floured board, use a rolling pin to roll out each dough ball to at least eight inches in diameter. You can't use a tortilla press because of the elasticity of the dough. Cook the tortillas on an iron griddle over medium heat, as you would corn tortillas.

With this same recipe my mamá would sometimes make *sopaipillas*. First she would roll one-and-a-quarter-inch balls of dough very thin, slice them pizza-style into four pieces, and then fry the wedges. After draining these puffy delicacies, she would roll them in sugar and cinnamon or pour honey on them. You can also make whole wheat tortillas, but don't try to fry these for sopaipillas; the dough is too coarse.

Once you know the beauties of both corn and flour tortillas, you may have trouble deciding which you prefer. Your choice will depend partly on tradition (some recipes call for a particular type) and partly on your mood. If you are a health-food addict, you will be pleased to hear that the corn tortilla has no salt, saturated fats, or preservatives. Weight watchers should know that depending on size, the average corn tortilla has thirty-five to fifty calories, while a flour tortilla has twenty-three to sixty-five calories, depending again on size and how much lard is used. Store-bought tortillas tend to have less lard. By comparison, a half-inch slice of white bread has seventy calories. As you can see, you are better off with a tortilla.

Consuming Passions

When I was in the service and the only tortillas I could get were Ashley's canned brand from El Paso, my mother took pity on me and mailed fresh ones special delivery. That was twenty-five years ago, when special delivery was actually special and delivered. I appreciated the homemade tortillas so much that she offered to get me my great-aunt's recipe for tortilla cookies, but I waited too long to accept her offer. Tía Nina died last year at the age of ninety-four, taking the recipe with her. I can't share the tortilla cookie recipe, but I can do the next best thing and pass along these other family favorites.

Tostadas

In Mexican homes it is the custom to save all the day-old tortillas and pan-fry them. Presto! Tostadas (tostaditas, if they're small). This is why there is always a bowl of tortilla chips and hot sauce in Mexican restaurants. Of course, this is not to say that they are made from yesterday's tortillas.

Tortilla Soup

My mother's favorite way of using stale tortillas was in tortilla soup. First she made chicken or beef broth with tomatoes and spices for flavor. She always added a dash of cumin, which makes the difference with lots of Mexican soups. The tortillas are diced, fried, drained, and added to the bowls of soup at the last moment so the chips won't get soggy.

Albóndigas

Another great recipe for leftover tortillas is *albóndigas*, Mexican meat matzo balls. Say you have a dozen stale tortillas. Grind them with a mortar and pestle or in a food processor, or for more authenticity use a *metate*, a Mexican mortar made from a volcanic stone. Then add one egg, one-quarter teaspoon salt, one-half cup of grated white cheese (such as farmer's cheese), and one-half cup of hot milk, and stir. Refrigerate the dough for an afternoon or overnight to allow the tortilla particles to soften. Later that day or the next morning knead the dough well and add more milk if necessary. From this dough make a dozen small balls, the albóndigas. In a frying pan heat the lard (other shortening will do, but lard is more authentic) and fry the albóndigas until they are golden brown. Drain well and they are ready to be added to soup; chopped cilantro makes an attractive topping.

Tío Pancho and the Margarita

*W*e are probably the only family in the world that has a taboo on one of the most popular mixed drinks, the margarita. When my aunts, uncles, and cousins get together in Juárez or El Paso and my Aunt Bibi is present, no one, out of respect, drinks margaritas, or much less mentions the name. My Aunt Bibi, you see, was married to Francisco Morales, the man who invented the margarita. They were divorced many years ago, and by coincidence he married a girl named Margarita.

I went to visit tío Francisco a couple of years ago. He was working as a milkman in El Paso and getting up at four in the morning. He used to be a well-known bartender, some say the best in Mexico, and is credited with having invented other drinks, such as the Conga Cooler, the Pancho López, and the Viejito.

"Fourth of July 1942," he recalled. "It's so vivid in my mind. A woman came into Tommy's Place there in Juárez one afternoon and asked for a magnolia. It was a popular ladies' drink in those days, but I forgot what it contained. I knew it had Cointreau, lime, and ice, but couldn't remember what kind of liquor. So I used tequila.

"'This isn't a magnolia, but it's very good,' she told me. 'What is it called?' There was already a drink named the Texas Daisy, so I thought the translation of daisy would be appropriate. 'Oh, I'm sorry. I thought you had asked for a margarita.' I lied to keep my professional pride." And so the margarita was born.

My Uncle Pancho, who was only twenty-four at the time, continued to serve margaritas to the Fort Bliss soldiers who crowded into Tommy's Place and demanded all kinds of cocktails during the Second World War. He invented many drinks in honor of various girlfriends or fighter planes, such as the P-38.

The first margarita was served from a shaker into a six-ounce champagne glass. It was not filled to the brim. This is in very bad taste, my uncle says. The ingredients were: ⅘ tequila, ⅕ Cointreau, half a lime, and chipped ice. Because that was too strong, it was soon modified to ⅔ tequila, ⅓ Cointreau, and half a lime with chipped ice. Nowadays, most people use another triple sec instead of Cointreau. Both are made from fermented orange peels.

There was a popular drink called the Sidecar that had a half-moon of sugar on the rim of the glass. Since tequila goes with salt and lime, my tío Pancho decided to wet the outer rim of the glass with a lime and sprinkle a full moon of salt. He is revolted when bartenders bury the whole rim of the glass in a dish of salt. Another modern bad habit is the use of shaved ice, he says. "It dilutes the liquor too much. You lose the bouquet."

Eventually, after his invention and divorce, my tío met his present wife, Margarita. When they were courting, he told her, "I'm a bartender, not a poet, so I named a drink after you."

After moving to the United States, tío Pancho entered a Tequila Sauza mixed-drink contest for bartenders who belonged to a union. He sent them his margarita recipe but was disqualified because the contest was for Mexican residents only. Now Tequila Sauza representatives come to exhibit at the National Juárez Trade Fair every year, and they always invite him to have a drink. Remembering the disqualification, he orders a Scotch.

He showed me a copy of *National Geographic* magazine where Margarita Sauza is asked if the margarita was named in her honor. She answers no, and says it was invented by a man in northern Mexico.

When my wife and I were in El Paso recently, we did not see my uncle but we visited my Aunt Bibi and went shopping with her in Juárez. While the women bought groceries, I chose three bottles of liquor, including one of margarita. But as I walked toward the checkout with my purchases, I suddenly remembered the taboo. I put the margarita back on the shelf and made another choice.

The Great Taco War

*I*n Redwood City, California, when the Mexican flag was hoisted over the Taco Bell fast-food restaurant, the local Mexican-American business community was angered and the flag was taken down. Taco Bell is determined to make inroads into the Mexican community through its culture and economies.

Tacos have become the hamburger's stiffest competitor as this country's favorite fast food. As of 1990, Taco Bell had already jumped ahead of McDonald's. But forget hamburgers for a couple of minutes. Today Taco Bell has not only infiltrated the barrios but has even opened its first restaurant in, of all places, Mexico City.

A Colonel Sanders Kentucky Fried Chicken restaurant in Beijing or a McDonald's in Moscow does not seem as strange as a Taco Bell in the capital city of Mexico. I was already aghast when a Taco Bell was built in San Francisco's Mission District, where salsa music, bright murals, and traffic lights compete for attention, and where there is at least one taqueria every two blocks.

In the Mission District, taquerias are San Francisco's nouvelle eating places. Yuppies and business executives from uptown dine elbow-to-elbow with cholos and other Latinos on exquisitely prepared designer tacos and burritos made from charbroiled diced beef, chicken, pork, corned beef, tongue, brains, or veggies for vegetarians.

The taquerias are so popular that most customers are veritable connoisseurs of which is the talk o' the town. So it was brazen of Taco Bell to come into the Mission District and sell their mild imitations of the real thing. Still, they sold tacos to Chicanos and other Latinos in the barrio like they were going out of *estilo*.

¿Qué pasó? Taco Bell was competing with what some call the best taquerias north of the border. The news was so disturbing that the "godfather of the Mission District," Rene Yañez, took me to see it. "You gotta write about this," he said.

This fast-food restaurant came complete with California Mission-style architecture and a yellow plastic bell. It was surrounded by a beauty salon, a Chinese restaurant, a hardware store, and a mattress store. In the morning, the Taco Bell corner serves as an unemployment line for Latinos in search of a day's work.

Taco Bell does brisk business. What seemed like a crowd from the outside was a slow, meandering line, Disneyland-style. This was better than walking into a burger place and wondering which line would move faster, only to get behind the guy ordering twenty Big Macs, ten regular fries, ten large fries, five diet Cokes, five regular Cokes, ten malts, and two coffees for a hungry work crew.

The Taco Bell menu can be a mystery if one is not familiar with the renamed food items. They can even puzzle a bicultural person. What's an Enchirito? "A combination burrito and enchilada," the manager answered, half bored and following his response with a half-accusing glance at my ignorance. I had envisioned a half-burrito, half-enchilada transplant and felt the heartburn coming on.

They also featured Mexican pizza, which was a flat flour tortilla smothered with refried beans and topped with ground beef, cheese, and shredded lettuce. But what were Cinnamon Crispas? They were similar to *buñuelos*, fried flour tortillas generously sprinkled with sugar and cinnamon.

Other items on the menu included the Nachos Bell Grande, Taco Bell Grande, and, of course, the kid's Fiesta Meal, which seemed incomplete without a piñata. They also listed steak fajitas and chicken fajitas, complete with the helpful phonetic spelling—"Fa-hee-tahs."

I ordered two tacos prepared with prefabricated hard tortilla shells at room temperature. Rene ordered the Mexican pizza. The meat was luke-warm and the cheese and shredded lettuce were cold. Halfway through the taco, the shell crumbled between my fingers and landed on my tray. Rene laughed, and then I realized the reason for the plastic fork. When I finally got to taste my "taco," it was different and tasty in a funny sort of way. There is something surreal about having to tear a little plastic package with one's teeth in order to get to a salsa that is more mild and sweet than hot. Give me a dark green fresh jalapeño to sink my teeth into any day.

Orders are served in under five minutes and placed on a plastic tray with a paper placemat headlined "The Border Run." It depicts an open highway in the desert leading to a Taco Bell and surrounded by highway signs that tell you to "Crack It, Bust It, Jump It, Snap It, or Cross It." This, of course, is a subtle reference to crossing the border illegally or jumping a once-proposed fifteen-mile ditch south of San Diego. The hidden message is that eating at Taco Bell can be not only a treat but a real, live Indiana Jones adventure.

And who is the clientele in this Taco Bell in the barrio? *Los pobres*, poor people, seniors on fixed retirement incomes, and immigrants who have "jumped, crossed, or beat it" to this side. At 59 cents a taco, where else can a poor family eat for less than ten dollars with free drink refills? Where else can Latino teenagers hang out to socialize? Not at the barrio taquerias where tacos start at $1.50 each.

A typical day will find the outdoor seating of Taco Bell filled with Latinos of various ages. On one occasion a group of *batos locos*, crazy dudes, yelled at each other across the tables using foul español. This didn't faze the older and younger women, who kept right on conversing and eating. On a second visit, there was a whole day-care nursery of some eighteen small fries, I mean, four- and five-year-old children. Where else could they have afforded lunch?

In other parts of the city you can see the taco price war between Taco Bell and Jack in the Box: 59 cents a taco, 49 cents a taco, 39 cents a taco, three for a dollar . . . There's no end to the sales.

Not to be outdone, the Kentucky Fried Chicken franchise in the Mission District raised a banner selling: "Oven roasted chicken with tortillas and salsa!" But finally the Colonel chickened out. The pollo fare was only on a trial basis. Colonel Sanders may have been making a lot of yuan in downtown Beijing, but in the Mission District he was losing dinero to tacos. The growing popularity of fast Mexican food in barrios such as the Mission District will be a significant turning point in the national taco war. Our burritos and tacos are not only the real thing but our first line of defense.

The fast-food enterprise is cashing in on the unabashed sale of Anglicized and commercialized Mexican food to low-income Latinos, and the message is clear. "Hey! We can't make it as good as you can, but we can sure sell it faster and cheaper than you." Some hard-shelled Chicanos and Mexicanos wouldn't be caught dead in one of these Taco Bells. For others, though, an empty stomach and pocketbook do not distinguish the "real" thing.

The Joy of Jalapeños

*I*n Mesoamerican cuisine, nothing compares with the gastronomic ecstasy that a hot jalapeño adds to the enjoyment of Mexican food. The piquant sensation on the tongue, the itch and tingling on the scalp, the beads of sweat on the forehead, the clearing of the sinus passages, and the fogging of eyeglasses are all part of a cultural ritual in the ultimate Mexican eating experience.

Even among Mexicanos, many are invited but few are chosen to enjoy this seemingly masochistic practice of setting your mouth afire while nourishing your body and enjoying the food.

Like so many of my paisanos, I cannot, for the life of me, enjoy any type of food, whether it be gringo, Jewish, or Italian, without a good hot salsa, *jalapeños en escabeche, pico de gallo, chile de arbol, hecho al molcahete,* crushed red pepper, Tabasco sauce, Louisiana hot sauce, *chile habanero,* or just a fresh, dark green jalapeño.

Chile might have formed me into the kind of person I am, sometimes hot-tempered and passionate. Back home at the family table, we could always count on having two types of tortillas, *de maíz* or *harina,* beans, and three types of chiles: *rojo*, *verde*, and *fresco*—red, green, and the fresh, unadulterated jalapeño in all of its luscious, dark green subtlety. Sometimes we had *hueros*, blonde yellow peppers, very innocent looking but just as deadly as the green ones. Other times we might have serranos, but while they were hot, they lacked the flavor of the jalapeño.

Father always went for the hottest one. If it was a dud, he would ask for another. Sometimes one chile was so hot that it took two meals to finish. Those gems were rare.

There is a whole process to evaluating a *salsa de chile*, and it's not by looking at the label to see if it was made in New Yawk City or Santone. First you study it in the bowl. If it's too tomatoey, it was probably made for tender tongues. With a spoon, you sift it to check its consistency, the spices used, and how it was made: by roasting, cooking the peppers in water first, chopped in the blender of a Cuisinart. But the best flavor comes from the *molcahete*. After the chiles have been roasted and peeled, they are ground on a stone mortar. The stone flavor and the ground seeds add a special earthy taste.

A trained and experienced olfactory sense will tell you if it is hot or not. The fourth and final step in the examination is putting a small amount on the back of your hand and tasting it. Some like to use a corn chip, but such interference dilutes the flavor. You need to know exactly how hot it is so you can add the correct amount to your food.

That ritual of tasting has all but disappeared with the sale of commercially made mild, medium, hot, and very hot sauces. But there is nothing like homemade salsa. Contrary to popular belief, Mexican food is not hot, which is why salsas were created.

Tastes and preferences are personal, but I frown on restaurants that load the salsa with *cominos*, tomatoes, and onions. The taste of those ingredients remain with you more than the jalapeño taste. Chiles, whether they be jalapeños or serranos, have their own peculiar tastes that should be enhanced, not hidden.

Nothing was more painful when I left home for the air force than to be served bland, gringo military food. That's where I developed a taste for common ordinary black pepper, Louisiana hot sauce, or Tabasco. The SOS eggs and sausage needed help. Since my departure from home I have forever yearned for salsas and fresh jalapeños.

From time to time when I was in the military, mother would send me care packages of canned jalapeños en escabeche or other forms of canned chile salsas. I was desperate and celebrated those few hot times, shedding tears of jalapeño joy with other Chicano buddies.

In Spain we introduced young Spanish women to what we told them were Mexican pickles. They had never heard of a jalapeño before. Their faces turned neon red.

In Zaragoza, Spain, a woman friend invited me to her home for dinner. Without jalapeños she made a sauce from crushed red pepper, spices, and cognac. It was a fine moment in European gastronomic ingenuity.

My addiction for jalapeños is such that I confess to have eaten at exclusive restaurants and attended formal banquets with fresh jalapeños in my coat pocket. Banquet food can be boring, and asking for the Tabasco sauce is a faux pas. If sitting with people who find such conduct reproachable, I simply cup my hands around the pepper and bite into it from time to time without their ever knowing. I have been caught only once, and another time a table companion confessed to me he wished he had brought jalapeños with him too.

Once I gave a humorous presentation at the annual California Rural Legal Assistance fund-raising banquet. Before the presentation, while people were eating, I went around offering fresh jalapeños to go with their bland chicken. Some Hispanics were insulted and blushed, while some Chicanos were delighted and blushed only after they bit into their dark green hot peppers.

To get the most out of a fresh jalapeño, especially one that has been refrigerated, it is necessary to get its hot juices flowing. Cup the pepper with both hands and blow warm breath onto it while rolling it between your palms. This is called "getting the jalapeño angry." It's supposed to get hotter if you curse it in Spanish.

Of course, there are many kinds of chiles, but the jalapeño is the king and named after the small town of Jalapa, Veracruz, where the character of the people is both piquant and picaresque. This is the same region that originated the dance and hot musical number "La Bamba," perhaps inspired by the effects of a jalapeño.

Much more can be said about this phallic plant food that can bring tears to the most macho of machos. With the Chicano Movement, artists turned the jalapeño into an icon, a symbol, and image representing the culinary, piquant, and humorous aspect of Mexican culture. In a famous Mexican ballad, "La Llorona," the male singer cries out, "Yo soy como el chile verde, llorona, picoso pero sabroso"—I am like the green chile, wailing woman, hot but delicious!

The curative qualities and other little-known facts of the jalapeño and its pepper cousins are many.

Menudo, Mexican tripe soup, known as the national Mexican breakfast of champions, is known to cure hangovers. The truth: It is the chile in the menudo that activates the juices in your system and fights against alcohol dehydration.

According to Dr. T. F. Burks of the University of Arizona Health Sciences Center, hot peppers contain capsaicin, a chemical that is responsible for the piquancy and can effectively relieve certain types of pain. Like acupuncture, capsaicin blocks the nerve pathways that carry pain signals to the brain in chronic conditions such as pinched nerves and tumors.

A chile a day keeps the doctor away. U.S. government studies show that people living in the Southwest have the lowest death rate from heart disease and cancer in the United States. One doctor, Lora M. Shields, reported that chile may help rid the body of enough fats to lower cholesterol.

When the diet of the Otomi Indians of central Mexico was studied by the Massachusetts Institute of Technology, their diet was found to be much more nutritious than the diet of a group of U.S. town dwellers. Since pre-Columbian times, the chile has been used in folk medicine as a remedy for inflamed kidneys, chills, heart pains, and tumors.

One ounce of chile contains as much as twenty thousand units of vitamin A, which is twice the minimum daily requirement. Fresh chiles have even higher levels. One hundred grams of Texas green chile contain 235 mg of vitamin C, while a California orange has but 49 mg. Calcium content in chiles is also high.

According to *Albuquerque Living*'s Life Style poll in March 1987, Anglos prefer green chile and Latinos love red chile.

Curanderas, folk medicine healers, believe that hot chile peppers and salt on top of a cross made of nails can ward off witches.

In 1937 Dr. Albert Szent-Györgyi was awarded the Nobel Prize in science for his studies of vitamin C in paprika peppers, a cousin of the jalapeño.

Cold, insensitive feet or those with poor blood circulation have been revived by sprinkling socks or nylons with hot, red chile powder.

In 1982, astronaut Bill Lenoir had an upset stomach that was linked to the jalapeño peppers he had carried into orbit. Eating and digesting chile is a process that takes some getting used to, especially in outer space. Start off slowly and build up. Find a chile that you like but that doesn't act like acupuncture, blocking your enjoyment of the food. But once you are *enchilado*, try to remain calm and not panic. People have gotten hurt when they run, trip, bump their heads, or poison themselves by drinking the first liquid they see. Your best bet is dairy products: milk, sour cream, ice cream . . .

Boy Eating Book. Poetry, like bread, is for the people. That don't mean you're always gunna like it.

Dr. Paul Rozin of the University of Pennsylvania psychology department conducted a study of cultural food preferences, particularly for the chile pepper. According to Dr. Rozin, chile aids digestion by stimulating gastric secretion and salivation, and helps to cool off the body by causing the face to sweat.

Furthermore, Dr. Rozin suspects that hot peppers trigger the release of endorphins, which are natural opiates of the brain, into the chile eater's system. So it may be that my addiction to jalapeños is caused not by cultural affiliation or heredity, but by endorphins.

Spilling the Beans

*E*at your beans!"

I hated beans; I ate them all the time. We had beans in the morning, at noon, and at night.

"Eat your beans!" "Finish your beans!"

We ate them as freshly made *frijoles de la olla*, we ate them in different recipes: *frijoles borrachos, frijoles charros, frijoles sencillos* . . . We ate *enfrijoladas*, like enchiladas but soaked in beans instead of chile; we had *tacos de frijoles*, bean burritos, *tostadas de burritos*, refried bean sandwiches, and even matzos or bagels smothered with refried beans. We scrambled them with eggs, we ate them with diced jalapeños, nopalitos, chorizo, melted cheese . . . You name it. We ate frijoles when its soup thickened. We ate them when the refried beans had just about dried up.

Enter any Mexican home and you can tell by the smell if there is a fresh pot of beans on the stove. The aroma is unmistakable. A pot of freshly made beans is a delectable dish. Well cooked, beans will just about melt in your mouth. Immediately after cooking, add oregano, cilantro, onions, or even Parmesan cheese to individual servings for an exquisite culinary experience. For many of us it is our invariable soup du jour. Some people will add a can of beer when the beans are cooking. And the second time they are warmed up some people add milk or cream or cheese.

But somehow, grandmother's beans always tasted better, and my mother's were also good but different from my aunts' and my mother-in-law's. It was the water! Or a mystery that will forever remain a *secreto*. And there were times when my Mexican aunts would open up a quart of beans the way you opened a glass liter of milk. Some entrepreneur began marketing it as an indispensable common staple like milk.

And once in a while my mother made them my favorite way, as a dessert, as a sweet pudding, similar to chocolate. Gently cooking them with sugar instead of salt, she blended them and added cinnamon and a touch of vanilla, sometimes raisins. It was better than chocolate pudding. Beans were not only economical but versatile. However, we did have a choice at mealtime: It was eat them or *nada*!

We also feasted on many other kinds of legumes, such as *lentejas*, which my mother called *frijolito del niño Dios*, because Baby Jesus was supposed to have eaten them. How could we refuse? There were navy beans, garbanzos, lima beans, kidney beans, black beans, and pinto beans. Whether we liked them or not, we ate them all.

Easy to prepare, the most essential and critical part was to thoroughly clean them of hard little rocks that could easily demolish your molars, incisors, or front teeth. But beans also had fun uses. Small bean bags were fun to throw and play catch with. Peashooters had their season. Beans were what we played Lotería with, the Mexican bingo game. "El cazo!" And we would put a pinto bean on that picture.

Beans could also be dangerous. Little kids would put a dry pinto bean up their nose. Sometimes they said nothing until the bean softened, grew, and sprouted like a sponge, then had to be extracted by the family doctor.

While I was being forced to eat my beans, little Johnny and Susie were being forced to eat their spinach. As the all-American vegetable, it was supposed to make them strong like Popeye the Sailor Man. In Crystal City, Texas, the supposed spinach capital of the world and the stronghold of Chicano activism in the late sixties, they even erected a statue of Popeye.

I liked spinach, but no one ever told us the beans packed more power than spinach. We should have brought out Freddy Frijol, who would have whipped Popeye. The difference at the Battle of the Alamo was the difference between *espinacas* and frijoles. Mexico won! Remember the Alamo!

High in iron, beans form an essential part of the mechanism in the blood that helps supply oxygen to body cells, aids in respiration and energy production. It's also an excellent source of fiber and rich in minerals, including calcium, phosphorus, magnesium, niacin, thiamine, riboflavin, B vitamins, and zinc. It helps in blood clotting. Beans, frijoles, legumes, those dehydrated pods of edible food that turn soft and nutritious when cooked, go back to the Bronze Age, thus the reason for our color. A couple of thousand years before Christ, they were already grown by Egyptians, who claimed they had a mystical power and offered them in their rituals to the deceased.

The Romans determined the guilt or innocence of a man on trial with beans. Jurors would cast a white bean for innocence and a black or red bean for guilt. The status of beans among Romans is found in the names of prominent ancient families: Fabius was named after the fava bean, Lentulus after the lentil, Piso for the pea, and the most distinguished, Cicero, was named after the chickpea.

Then there was Judge Roy Bean (1825?–1904) a West Texas saloon keeper, coroner, and justice of the peace on the West Texas frontier. He had his hands full with his six-guns and a town filled with gamblers, rustlers, and thieves. He was the "law west of the Pecos," who once fined a corpse $40 for carrying a concealed weapon. In more modern times, another Texan, U.S. astronaut Alan LaVern Bean, piloted the lunar module *Intrepid* on the Apollo 12 mission and in November of 1969 made man's second moon landing. Last but not least is my friend Frijol, who has yet to do anything of such magnitude, but his life isn't over.

One historical dish stands out: *moros y cristianos*, Moors and Christians. That's what you call a plate of white rice and black beans, referring to the African Moors who occupied white Spain for close to eight hundred years until they were expelled in 1492. In Nicaragua, a similar dish is called *gallo pinto*.

Other Spanish names for frijoles abound: *júdias de león*, *habichuelas*, *alubias*, and *habas*. As kids we would change *frijoles* to a more Chicano-sounding *firoles* or *balas*; *un plato de balas* was a deadly "plate of bullets." Beans are rich in nutrition, but many people shy away from them because of their gas-producing properties, something that can easily be remedied. (One way is to repeatedly discard the water. First, let the beans soak temporarily or overnight and then throw out the water. Boil them and throw out the water again. When adding new water, boil it first if you want your pinto beans to retain a pink color, otherwise they turn dark. Another remedy is to use a commercial food additive known as Beano and follow its directions. *¡Muy importante!*)

Long thought to be the staple of peasants, who would have thought they would be served in fancy restaurants or banquets? Imagine a maitre d' reciting the soup du jour as *frijoles de la olla* or a *paté de refritos*. But there are very exclusive restaurants that serve these dishes. Between San Francisco and San Diego it has become part of the new California cuisine.

Some people eat chicken and burp beans, so goes the Mexican proverb, "Comen pollo y erutan frijoles!" From the children's story about Jack and the Beanstalk to Miguel de Cervantes Saavedra's immortal *Don Quixote de la Mancha*, beans have risen to the highest levels of the literary classics.

Native to North and South America, many beans were domesticated by the Incas of Peru. Easier to cultivate in poorer soil than corn, they can be dried and stored for long periods of time.

But the beans that will spill from this book are beans that have boiled for over five hundred years. Not a melting pot but a kettle filled with black beans, white beans, red kidney beans, cranberry beans, coffee beans, navy beans, and pinto beans.

Spilling the beans is about disclosing, divulging, revealing, confessing, and publishing pods of truth, facts of integrity, humor, and pathos. Spilling them, hell! We are throwing them up in the air.

In Defense of the Jalapeño and Other Chiles

A cartoon in the *New Yorker* shows a smiling Eskimo street vendor selling blubber in midtown Manhattan, while a wrapped-up Euro-American walks by in the snow. Humorous though it may be, the cartoon also carries a clear and loud message about the infusion of exotic third-world foods not only on the streets of New York but throughout the country.

As salsa outsells ketchup and Taco Bell outsells McDonald's, the latest wave is the introduction of more authentic Mexican restaurants. A little too smug and comfortable with the growing availability of the real thing, we should have expected the competition to come up with something.

So it was no surprise that a recent small article in the *San Francisco Chronicle* was headlined "Hot Chili Peppers May Be Carcinogenic." The Cox News Service article stated that some "epidemiologists" from Yale University and the Mexico National Institute of Public Health "had concluded" that chile peppers "may be" carcinogenic, cancer producing. Laboratory experiments with animals and cells in test tubes had already found that capsaicin, the heat-producing agent in the peppers, is a carcinogen.

Dr. Robert Dubrow, a Yale Medical School epidemiologist, studied the incidence and distribution of stomach cancer and the eating habits of one thousand residents in Mexico City.

Mexico City? It's the biggest city on earth, with more than twenty million souls and over twenty-five million projected by the year 2000. With all the smog, congestion, and earthquakes that afflict its residents, why they didn't study people in rural areas or a more sedate and relaxed Mexican town, like Brownsville or some other town on the border, is a convenient mystery. They didn't have to go to Mexico City, unless they were after particular findings.

According to their studies, heavy consumers of hot chile peppers were seventeen times more likely to have stomach cancer than those who never eat hot peppers at all. Even people who considered themselves "medium" eaters were four times more likely to have stomach cancer. But what role did smog, earthquakes, and big-city nerves have in causing this?

Of course the two most interesting words in the headline and the article are "may be." The article stated their conclusion that chile peppers "may be" carcinogenic. Are they or are they not? The conclusion is "Maybe!" They weren't sure but felt compelled to broadcast their iffy conclusion.

How or why (two important questions for journalists) this study was thought up and who funded it should also be newsworthy. According to the article, per capita consumption of chile peppers in this country more than doubled from 1982 to 1992. Pace Picante Sauce, made in Santone, is a big seller in Mexico. Was this funded by a McDonald's, or was the Ketchup Association trying to catch up? And so how many readers will believe and begin to boycott jalapeños due to this inconclusive study while they continue to consume carcinogenic California table grapes?

Cesar Chavez had led a five-year boycott of California table grapes when he died. For years, the United Farm Workers have been sounding a warning about the danger of agricultural pesticides. Some three hundred thousand farmworkers a year are stricken with pesticide-related illnesses. Childhood cancer and birth defects have reached epidemic proportions in many San Joaquin Valley towns. Yet you don't see Yale University epidemiologists coming to study this. You don't see the Mexican Institute for Public Health trying to protect their poor emigrant farmworkers from the pesticides in this country. Not until the mainstream majority in this country begins to feel the effects will any study be done. Until then, it's only affecting Mexican migrant workers, so who cares?

Meanwhile, a month after the inconclusive jalapeño scare, Florida legislators were trying to consider a bill that would give farmers the right to sue anyone who defames their crops. Criticize a cucumber, badmouth a bell pepper, insult a lettuce, and you may have a day in court with possible jail time.

Under such a proposed law, farmers could slap a lawsuit on anyone who publicly states that a Florida-grown food product is unsafe for human consumption without reliable scientific facts to back up their claim.

A year before these two articles appeared, there was a study out of Stanford University's Center for Research in Disease Prevention, which stated that the traditional diet of Mexican Americans is healthier than that of Euro-Americans. That totally goes against the grain of what we have heard all our lives, but according to the study, Mexican Americans eat less cheese, fried foods, red meat, and cured meat such as hot dogs, and add less fat to food after cooking. They also eat more healthy foods high in carbohydrates and fiber, such as rice, corn, and dried beans.

According to the study, the more acculturated you become, the more you take on the Euro-American's bad habits. In July of 1994 yet another highly publicized study concluded that Mexican food is high in fat and cholesterol. The contradictions of these studies are confusing, but it appears that Americans can create Mexican fast foods that are less healthy by preparing beans cooked with lard, fried meats, and by adding an abundance of sour cream, guacamole, and cheeses. It seems untrue because this isn't really the authentic cuisine of Mexico. All these contradictory news items go to prove only one thing, that with the right funding and an abiding press you can prove just about anything. ¡Viva el jalapeño!

Postscript

Months after writing this, and a whole lifetime as a jalapeño consumer, aficionado, advocate, and activist, I was diagnosed with an abdominal tumor.

My alternatives here could have been to be obstinate on the unconvincing studies of one thousand chile pepper eaters in Mexico City, a megalopolis of twenty million. Natives of Veracruz, home of the jalapeño, or people from the northern state of Chihuahua consume more hot peppers than Chilangos, Mexico City natives.

However, people will respectfully believe whatever they want to believe. Some friends pointed out that maybe it was the jalapeños that caused my tumor. Without dismissing that possibility, I'm also acutely aware of other probable causes. I even believe that jalapeños have antioxidants that prevent cancer. However, "maybe" like radiation treatment for cancer, too much of a good thing or a bad thing can cause cancer.

I won't live my life observing all the "maybe" caution signs. So I will eat jalapeños again, but moderately and mildly. Besides, what kind of a Mexicano or Chicano would not love and defend jalapeños?

Litany for the Tomato

For the sweetness of a tomato
    you need:
    one Chicano farmworker,
    twelve hours in the field,
      loyalty to the earth,
        your soul on the mountain,
          far from the streets,
            love for the valleys,
              songs of color,
                pain and love,
                  guitars in the nights,

recalling the jarochos,
    dreams in the winds,
      lulling the dead,
    a brilliant sun,
      much stamina,
        footprints in the fields

of miles of chiles,
burning their backs
and   dragging

their skirts,
saints in corners
of cardboard houses,
sweat in their blood,
slicing the hunger,
and the wire;
seeds in their hands
sewing new dreams,
in the palms of their hands,
that bleed and paint
one sweet tomato.

Berta Crocker's
Bicentennial Recipe

Con tu filero,

----

cut along the dotted line

Don't wait for the light to change to brown.

Adentro you will find
Tres paquetes:
      One Red
      One White
      One Blue

Mézclalos . . .
          pero con huevos.

Stick it in the oven for 200 years.

Skool Daze

Un burrito de chorizo con huevos
        stained my brown paper bag y los kakis
            while Suzy looked on,
                her Roy Rogers lunchbox
                hanging and laughing
                      with peanut butter jelly sandwiches.

Y las suelas de mis calcos—the soles of my shoes
        are loose like my tongue
            and I sound like a horse when I run,
                if I don't trip first,
                    because they bought them at
Las Tres B,   since   they   were
bonitos, buenos y baratos.

    Memo got pissed
  porque la ticha had told him,
        "Tuck your shirt in!"
                and so he tucked in his guayabera.

El Pifas was punished
        for being bilingual
                and so he wrote a hundred times:
                        I will not speak Spanish.
                                I will not speak Spanish.
                                        I will not speak Spanish.
using three pencils at a time
        finishing in record time.

And Father Rowland,
        refusing holy communion to doña Tencha
        because she wore tennis shoes
        that were easy on her juanetes—corns.

And Billy liked
the patches on my pants
so his Mom put some patches
        on his new pants.

And my mother at night
recounting all about the 16th and the Cinco,
        de los Niños Heroes—the boy heroes
                and the great robbery.

While in skool,
I learn of Amerika,
        the pilgrims,
                Remember the Alamo!
                Remember the Maine!
                        Remember the Gringa!
                        Malinche!   Pocahantas!
                        and amber waves of grain
                                from sea to China, yes!

Yes! That good ole skool daze
calls me back again,
        and I'll be coming home,
                look away, look away, Aztlán!
                ¡Tan, tan!

PART SIX: *From His Sketch Pad*

Editor's note: Artists carry their sketch pads everywhere they go. They seem to have this need to draw whatever strikes them as powerful or beautiful or humorous; or perhaps they want to capture something just because of its symmetry or because an idea has come to them that they do not want to forget. The editors were honored to have had the opportunity to go through Burciaga's sketch pads, tens and tens of sketch pads full of drawings he had done over the years: informal sketches he created while hanging out with friends or waiting for a meeting or just dreamily doodling as he looked out a window. Some of the sketches we found were not so much in pads as they were drawn on any piece of paper he could find, including napkins and mathematical paper. The following are some selections that we found in his pads, none of which have ever been seen. Some of them are very basic, simple lines in the style of Matisse, which create an incredible feeling with a few strokes of a pen. Others are more complicated, more detailed, some of which he was clearly proud of, as he signed and dated them, perhaps anticipating using them in a future book. Of the hundreds of drawings, here we present to you only a few, in addition to the sketches we have sprinkled throughout this book. In a later section, "Friends," we include drawings he did when he was hanging out. He couldn't help it—he had to pick up pen and draw his friends.

Cool Vato. This sketch was found in one of those lined school notebooks that students use in Mexico. Burciaga blacked out a few squares and wrote the word "education" across the page, giving it a crossword puzzle–like feel. Then he put a cool guy sitting around in a "club-like atmosphere."

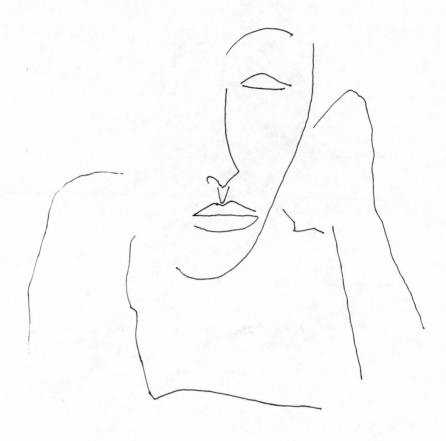

Matisse Sketch. This drawing is incredible in its simplicity, clearly evoking the work of Henri Matisse. With a few lines and curves, the artist breathes life into a personality.

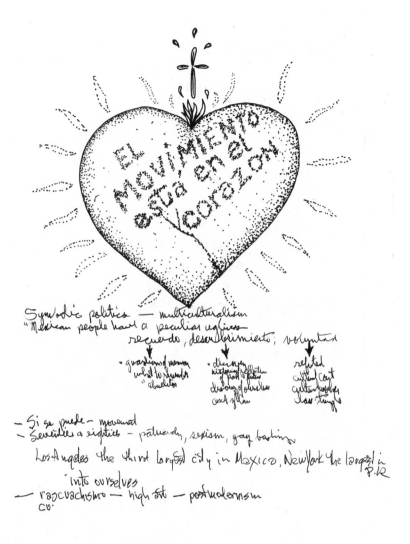

"El Movimiento está en el corazón." A peek into the mind of the artist, this image comes right from a sketch pad, a drawing perhaps he thought no one would ever see. It gives us a glimpse into his concern for the Chicano Movement, that is, activism for the Chicano/a people, and his dual voice as a visual artist and a man of letters.

MONUMENTAL BULLRING
EN
CENTROAMERICA

Ole!... The Greatest Show South Of The Border!

The USA's Greatest Matador

ENRIQUE KISSINGER

"El Gringo Loco"

With his 'cuadrilla' of commissioners will face 6 vicious and deadly bulls from:...

 **6**
TOROS

NICARAGUA
EL SALVADOR
GUATEMALA
HONDURAS
COSTA RICA
PANAMA

6
TOROS

Kissinger. Always the activist and humorist, the artist satirizes U.S. intervention in Central America as a macho act. Kissinger, the former U.S. secretary of state, takes on the bulls of Latin America. He is "the Crazy Gringo," the U.S.'s greatest matador (killer). He fights the six countries listed on the bottom of the image.

Dos lenguas
tres culturas

4 NOV 76

Dos Lenguas/Tres Culturas (Two Languages/Three Cultures). Although it's clear that the two languages are Spanish and English, it may be less clear what is meant by "three cultures." Burciaga is referring to the cultures of Mexico and the United States, out of which a third is created—the Chicano/a culture.

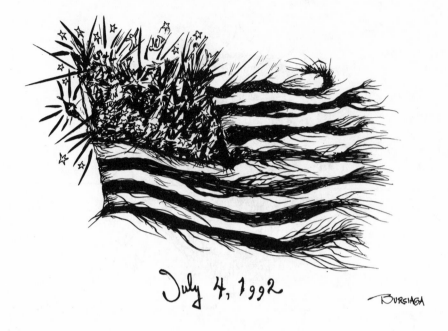

July 4, 1992. One's view of American pride can be more complex than "my country, love it or leave it." The country, as symbolized by the flag, has been through a lot, good and bad. Perhaps a country's greatness lies in both its colors and its tatters.

Typewriter Mouth. An imagistic rendering of the expression "a writer's voice"? Burciaga makes a visual pun.

PART SEVEN: *Friends*

Los amigos de mis amigos son amigos.
Any friend of yours is a friend of mine.

Amigo en la adversidad, amigo de realidad.
A friend in need is a friend indeed.

Al decir las verdades se pierden las amistades.
In telling the truth, friendships are lost.

La lengua del mal amigo más corta que el cuchillo.
The tongue of a false friend is sharper than a knife.

Handwritten on image: Lorna Dee Cervantez '76

Lorna Dee Cervantes and Alurista. Burciaga used to take his sketch pad with him to public events, readings, lectures, and rallies. He often pulled out the pad and drew his friends when they weren't looking. Here he has drawn the Chicano/a poets Lorna Dee Cervantes and Alurista, both of whom he respected.

ALURISTA

Purciaga

"FLORICANTO"
SAN-ANTO
1976

Esteban Villa

BURCIAGA 78

Esteban Villa and José Montoya. Esteban Villa and José Montoya were officers in the Rebel Chicano Art Front, aka the Royal Chicano Air Force, a group of Chicano artists and activists in Northern California. They were a crazy bunch, sometimes putting on impromptu shows and readings. José Montoya is also a poet, the author of the classic Chicano poem "El Louie."

José Montoya
'94

BURCIAGA

EL QUIXOTE DE AZTLÁN — Y QUE

RICARDO Sanchez
Floricanto III
San Anto
1976

Ricardo Sanchez. Here Burciaga has drawn a very aware Ricardo Sanchez (1941–1995), a Chicano poet who, like Burciaga, was from El Paso. This was sketched at the same event as the Cervantes/Alurista drawing, the Floricanto, a gathering of Chicano/a poets and musicians in San Antonio in 1976.

PART EIGHT: *The Temple Gang*

Growing Up Catholic Chicano in an Orthodox Jewish Synagogue on the Border

El amigo y el vino, antiguos.
With friends and wines, the older the better.

Amigo viejo, el mejor espejo.
An old friend is the best mirror.

Set'n the Scene

El Paso, Texas

I don't need to tell you how hot it gets in West Texas, so far west that sometimes you suspect you're in New Mexico or Old Mexico, there being no difference in the temperature or terrain of that vast open desierto where the sun and the sky swallow Chihuahua, Texas, and New Mexico whole, from breath-giving sunrises to breathtaking sunsets. It gets so caloroso that the flaming pavement will cook your huevos rancheros más pronto que quick and in the process curl your tortilla like a sea shell. The sun will sear your feet and fatigue you in no time curled.

Some fools will tell you it's a dry heat and not the humid heat of East Texas. It's the difference between cooking in an oven or hanging over boiling water. The choice is yours.

Either way takes some getting used to, but personally I'll take the dry huevos rancheros on a desert tortilla seashell. Once you get conditioned, the 115-degree heat will send shivers up and down your spine and only then will you have reached the "Nirvanic" level of appreciation and respect for what is *Kaliente*, with a capital "K."

Annually, just before noon, the local afternoon paper holds a contest to see who will predict the exact time the temperature will reach 100 degrees. When it does, the winner receives a cash prize and the paper carries a photo of someone frying eggs on a burning pavement like chicharras sizzling a serenade.

Before I get carried away on the topic, this genuine authentic and auspicious story was originally about the Temple Gang, a group of friends, batos locos, supposedly cool Chicano dudes, who hung out at a Jewish Orthodox synagogue in El Paso, Texas, during the pink and black fifties.

As I began to seriously consider this story I realized the strong role my father played and just as important the rich and interesting stories my whole family experienced living in a Jewish synagogue. Thus the story is a familiography, a biography of my parents and part biographical of my brothers and sisters.

The setting is a Jewish synagogue, named Congregation B'nai Zion, founded in 1927 on the Rio Grande border in the middle of a desert.

I can already hear some East Coast Jews softly musing, "Baba stories! A shul in the desert! Among Mexicans? Nechtiker tog—Nonsense!"

"¡Pero sí señores!" Israelites will tell you that the West Texas climate and terrain is more similar to theirs than New York's. Mormons believe Mexicanos to be one of the lost tribes referred to in the Old Testament.

This here story is about a man named Cruz, his familia, a group of Mexican-American youth, shaigetz—non-Jewish boys, searching and discovering their identities, their goals, long before the Chicano Movement, civil rights, affirmative action, discovering the border, border bordellos, drinking underage, working for judíos and mixing socially with their daughters, struggling with their lower-class status while living next to "Little Jerusalem," the upper-class Jewish neighborhood, and their krassavitseh—bellas mujeres—beautiful women, ¡Viva krassavitseh!

Thus we begin the story with how my father got to work and live in the basement of a Jewish synagogue on the desert outskirts of the West Texas town of El Paso.

Some names have been changed to protect the guilty, fools, and other inocentes, making no differentiation between the three.

On such a hot summer day in 1940 my jefito's temper was also seething. I never called my father "jefe," "jefito," or even thought of him as such. I do so now out of affection as a Chicano. My father always remembered his own father as "mi padre." Without variation, I always, respectfully, called him with an accent on the last *a*, Papá! I don't know what he would have done had I called him "Jefito" or "Daddy," or "Father." He might have given me a weird look, or he might have laughed through his open humor.

On that scorching day in 1940 his humor was steel tempered as he walked along the deserted road bordering the Rio Grande. After a back-breaking workday at the Southwestern Portland Cement Company, Cruz and eight other Mexicanos had been given their last paycheck and dismissed. It was dangerous, hazardous work alongside a booming monster ball, a machine with a flywheel, a flying belt with a whipping tail, and jaws that chewed up carload after carload of rock. The machine also pulverized the rock into a soft gray powder and then dropped it into deep storage bins, always ready to swallow the men who climbed up and down long flights of open steps hugging the walls. Sometimes, the men broke some of the rock with sledgehammers. The job was so brutal and dangerous and the salary so miserable that only Mexicanos were hired.

However, with the world on the brink of a second global war, they had been fired and the jobs had been redesignated as national defense employment. Only U.S. citizens were qualified: tough dumb gringos and semiassimilated Mexican Americans were offered these jobs with a smile. Cruz was offered the opportunity to keep his job if he became a U.S. citizen, but he refused. "I considered myself too Mexicano. Besides, I resented the ultimatum."

José Cruz felt the futile struggle of his life flowing down the Rio Grande alongside him. Oblivious to the crunch of his steps, Cruz walked past Smeltertown, the small barrio town across the highway from ASARCO, the American Smelting and Refining Company. He dreaded going home jobless. His pregnant wife of two years and a one-year-old daughter weighed on his mind. On that day as he trudged along the Rio, Cruz felt he had slipped all the way back to nada.

José Cruz Burciaga Zapata had been born May 3, 1905, on a rancho in Durango that soon became a town called Nazas where nada ever happened. Cruz was born with his mother's piercing blue eyes and blonde hair. From his elderly Indian father he had inherited his indigenous features, a handsome eaglelike nose. With his blonde hair and blue eyes, Cruz was a novelty. At seven months he was loaned to play the part of the infant Jesus for his first posada, a traditional Mexican Christmas pageant.

Ninety years later, his youngest son, Raul Enrique, was to discover a microfiche copy of his father's baptism certificate in the Family History Library of Salt Lake City, Utah, where over two million rolls of microfilm from around the world are archived.

It was more in the form of a register: "Fe de Bautismo Numero 638," dated the 31 de Mayo, 1905, in the church of Santa Ana de Nazas, hijo de Antonio Burciaga y Santos Zapata, paternal grandparents Francisco Burciaga y Cleofas Silva; maternal grandparents Feliziano Zapata y Docenta Valles.

The document was signed by padre Manuel Gallegos after advising godparents Francisco Peralta y María de los Angeles Zapata of their obligation as spiritual parents.

"Zapata!" Before we even knew who Emiliano Zapata was, our grandmother, abuelita Santos, proudly claimed Emiliano as a relative. Cómo no? she would challenge. "My Uncle Feliziano was his cousin." Later, the rest of the family could do nothing but laugh at her imagination.

After the layoff (from Southwestern Portland Cement Company), Cruz was offered a full-time job as janitor of a Jewish synagogue. After the dangerous, backbreaking national defense job at the cement plant, working for a more benevolent and peace-loving Jewish god was attractive, especially since the job came with a live-in residential apartment.

There was a serious dilemma in accepting the job. To work part-time in a Jewish synagogue was all right. Full-time employment and to live inside of a Jewish synagogue was a far more serious matter for a Catholic, even a semidevout Catholic, or for that matter for his wife, Guadalupe, a devoutly spiritual and religious Catholic. He would now work for the people who had killed Jesus Christ, a popular 1940 sentiment around the world.

Lupe urged Cruz to consult a priest. Cruz approached their wedding minister in Juárez. The priest listened and Cruz read the answer by the frown and slow shaking of the head. "¡De ninguna manera!—No way! How could you? There is no way you can conscientiously work for los judíos and maintain your Roman Catholic and Apostolic faith. Who killed Jesus Christ, huh? Can't you see what will happen? What kind of family do you expect to raise in a Jewish synagogue? A family of heretics? Huh? Answer me? Huh?"

Cruz didn't answer. He curtly thanked the priest and bid adios. Cruz was more angry and upset than convinced. How could he have expected the Holy Roman and Apostolic Church to sanction and allow such employment? He decided to get a second opinion, and so he approached a priest on the U.S. side of the border. Maybe they would be more open.

Cruz explained his predicament: no job, one little girl, and a second child due any day. Of course he wasn't going to forsake his Catholic faith, he reminded the priest. He attended Sunday Mass, had married in the church, and his sister was in the convent. The priest, a Mexican American, congratulated him and wished him the best in his new job.

With some reservations, Guadalupe accepted the decision. She was only too aware of their economic and home circumstances and left it in the hands of God.

On September 15, 1940, Cruz and Lupe moved into the basement apartment of Temple B'nai Zion with a one-and-half-year-old daughter, Margarita Guadalupe, and a month-old son, José Antonio. They had the barest of furniture. Guadalupe used the only bedroom in the back to hang and dry the clothes she washed by hand and made the living room their bedroom.

Armed with a bottle of blessed holy water, Guadalupe sprinkled the walls of her new home with Ave Marias y letanias a todos los santos in heaven above. At a later date, she would invite padre Balderrama, her sister's brother-in-law priest, to formally bless and sanctify the new home. It was not so much fear of the Jewish unknown as it was a holy tradition.

Guadalupe had already lived on the U.S. side of the border for one year, yet she felt even more miserably desolate and lonely in a culture twice removed from Mexico, only ten minutes away, but further inland, now completely cut off from her country.

For the first time in her thirty-two years she was not celebrating Mexico's Día de la Independencia. It was a Friday night and Cruz had to tend to the evening services. That night she was on the dark side of the río and discovered la luna, the moon, was Mexicana, now so far away. Guadalupe cried. She had forsaken her country, her family, and the Catholic god for a mortal man working in a temple for a Jewish god.

One consolation was also the reason for her tears, an upright Zenith radio with a nightly musical program called *Canciones inolvidables*— Unforgettable Songs. On the Mexican radio station, Equis E Jota, XEJ, the songs of Agustín Lara, Pedro Vargas, Pedro Infante, Jorge Negrete, and Libertad Lamarque resonated with the nostalgic pain of a home lost forever.

That first night in the temple she listened to El Grito, the annual Mexican cry for independence first uttered by Father Miguel Hidalgo on the night of September 15, 1812. And as he did every year the alcalde de Ciudad Juárez broadcast El Grito from his city hall balcony to hundreds of Juárez citizens cheering in the street below and hundreds more on the radio, including one former María Guadalupe Fernandez de Burciaga.

The pain she silently endured for the love of a man manifested itself in the way she brought up her children. They were to be not only educated but educados, personas de respeto e integridad, knowledgeable and proud of their Mexican blood and heritage. Mexican by birth and Americans by the grace of God.

María Guadalupe Fernandez

*H*ere was an honorable woman, a teacher who had not only taught her country's history and lived la Revolución de 1910, but had also suffered because of it. Here was a woman whose family lineage went back to one of the heroes of the Mexican War of Independence, José Antonio Torres. In the city of Guadalajara a statue commemorates and honors this Mexican hero. Streets throughout Mexico carry his name.

María Guadalupe Fernandez was born on September 15, 1907, in a small mining town called San Miguel, close to another silver mining town of Nieves, Zacatecas, in central Mexico, where she grew up. She was the oldest of four sisters and one brother.

María Guadalupe Fernandez also lost her father from the influenza. The conditions were the same throughout Mexico. When her father died, Alejandrina, a baby sister, was also ill with influenza. Everyone waited for her death so they could bury father and daughter in the same coffin, but the child survived to suffer life and die at a ripe old age.

Lupe remembers: "My mother was left with four small daughters and one son. De noche a día we were orphaned with nowhere to turn. We were down to our last centavos when tío Mundo, my mother's brother, already married and well established with a small store in Juárez, sent for us.'"

Lupe's family felt she had married beneath her class and potential. Courted by respectable suitors, prominent licenciados and doctores, she was not easily wooed. At thirty-two, beyond the common age for marriage, many had already consigned her to "dressing saints," a proverbial occupation for spinsters from respectable families. However, she was much too beautiful and sought after. And it was only Cruz who finally conquered her heart and won her love.

La familia Fernandez welcomed Cruz with polite decorum, but without gusto. Years later their children recall the obvious coolness he was treated with. To them, Cruz was nothing more than a fanfarrón, a popular and flashy dresser. José, as he was called by the family, with nothing more than a third-grade education, had succeeded in winning la mano de Lupe. For Lupe, a devout young woman, his buen corazón, y amor, convinced her that this would be the man she would spend the rest of her life with. Nonetheless, there was still something of a mystery. Cruz was not the religious type and he had picked up some very American ways, in particular his clothes. Unlike the other men who sought Lupe in matrimony, Cruz had nothing more than a good job in El Paso earning dólares.

At thirty-five, Cruz was no spring chicken. An honest and hardworking man, Lupe saw him as a good father, husband, and provider. His possessions were few. The man who had known destitute poverty gave everything away. As a single man working in Chicago, Gary, Indiana, California, and Colorado, Cruz had made enough money to send home to his mother and sisters. On one of his returns home, he had built them a stone house with a porch such as he had dreamed of in los Estates Unidos.

Now as he prepared for marriage he had little to show other than his good clothes. He was the proud owner of a five-inch-thick book entitled *Diccionario ilustrado de la lengua española* and a few other tomes of literature.

Guadalupe was a woman with principles and not easily swayed by the material wealth, power, and position of her other suitors. Cruz didn't have much to show in those aspects, but his love and sincerity won her over. They would live in Ciudad Juárez and raise a family. Cruz would continue to work in El Paso and she would raise the family.

But something happened after the first year. Whether the problem was working in El Paso and living in Ciudad Juárez isn't known. Cruz had lived on both sides of the border but was more familiar with the U.S. side. Once they were married, Cruz recognized that raising a family on the Americano side was more beneficial to the children.

At the same time Guadalupe was painfully aware of how emigrants to the United States were viewed in Mexico. They were traitors and their children would inherit the stigma of being called pochos, or worse, Chicanos. She was too painfully aware of how Mexican Americans had not only lost their roots, but shunned their roots, embarrassed by their own kind.

Guadalupe would give meaning to her children's lives. Determined to fortify her children with their idioma español e historia Mexicana, its war of independence from Spain.

She would constantly remind them that their new country was not an innocent new country. It had been stolen from Mexico, from indigenous people. No matter how many treaties and documents from here to the moon claimed Texas, Nuevo Mexico, Arizona, Nevada, and California as part and parcel of the United States of America, it was really part of Mexico. Its history, the names, and the people north of the Rio Grande would always haunt and remind her children to be proud Mexicanos!

Just as honestly, she also recognized and appreciated the Irish American priests and nuns, whose schools her children would be attending. Four blocks south of the synagogue was St. Patrick's Cathedral and Catholic grade school. The Sisters of Loretto would be indoctrinating her children in la santa iglesia católica, apostólica y romána. Whatever language, the Catholic faith was truly catholic, universal, she thought.

And they would also learn U.S. history, about George Washington and Thomas Jefferson and their war of independence from Britain. Her children would learn of the greatness de los Estados Unidos. She never doubted its greatness, but always questioned the morality of its history and relations with Mexico.

For now, Lupe's reality was living in a basement apartment as her new home. Again and again, she thought of how enormous the house was, though comfortable in such a big three-story building, occupying a quarter of a city block.

The shul was U-shaped with a patio in the middle. Built in 1928, the modern building was only twelve years old. Cruz would no longer need work in faraway Smeltertown. All he had to do was step outside the door of his home and there was his workplace.

Right above our home was the main temple that seated five hundred, including a balcony. Next to the altar was a door to Rabbi Roth's study with a formidable walk-in safe. On that same floor was also a one-room library and administrative office.

Next to the temple was a ballroom with a stage, a separate lounge next to a grand entrance, and a large kitchen with three big stoves. On the third floor was an all-purpose room with a smaller kitchen and more classrooms.

On the other side of our bedroom wall was a dark chapel. Outside our front door were three of eleven classrooms for Hebrew school. And in an even lower basement was a large basketball gym that was also fitted for gymnastics. Behind the gym lay a long unfinished bowling alley, a billiard room, and bathrooms with showers. In that lower basement was a boiler room with a gigantic gas furnace that distributed heat throughout the building via an artery of clanking pipes and radiators. The high Rocky Mountain desert mesa made Arctic winters possible. Without a temperature gauge, the furnace would be turned on until it got extremely hot, then turned off.

The hundreds of hiding places from the attic to the roof and the boiler room afforded us getaway hiding places. "We never played hide-and-seek because it was literally impossible to find someone," Raul remembers. "But it was great to play secret agent." For me, the sixties were the days of *Man from U.N.C.L.E.*, James Bond, *The Saint*, and *The Avengers*. The shul offered a terrific setting for secret agent games. My ancient brothers, fifteen years my senior, had to settle for fifties' cowboys and robbers. The closest they ever got to the real world on television was *I Led Three Lives*, an anti-communist television series during the cold war of the fifties. Johnny and I played Napoleon Solo or Agent 007. On any given day we saved the world from terrorist and un-American activities.

Close to the outskirts of town, our neighborhood was originally upper middle class, with empty desert lots next door and across the streets surrounding that block. Behind the faded orange brick Jewish temple was the El Paso Women's Center, an elegant dark gray brick building with white columns gracing the front entrance. A block behind was the combined Catholic Community Center and Cathedral High School.

Rabbi Joseph M. Roth

*R*abbi Joseph M. Roth was Ben Toyreh, a son of the Torah, a learned man, quiet and respected, a severe, stern, and strict Orthodox Jewish rabbi from another century, of relatively small height and build, close-cropped graying hair, and a thin mustache, I never saw him smile. He was also a professor of philosophy at Texas Western College. The adult congregation treated him with fear and respect. Hebrew school students shuddered at the thought of standing in front of a harsh disciplinarian.

Rabbi Roth had seen Cruz working part-time but had never said a word to him. When the congregation formally hired him, the rabbi called Cruz to his office the very first week. This was a new experience for Cruz, sitting in front of the rabbi in his office.

"You have been hired as the Shabbat goy of this temple and we welcome you with open arms. You are the janitor, the caretaker of this temple of God, and more than that: Zachor!—Remember always, the word *janitor* means "first," it means entrance. It comes from the same word as January.

You hold the key to this temple. You are the Shabbat goy, you are privileged among the gentiles. As the Shabbat goy you will perform those duties that are forbidden us on Shabbat by Talmudic law—turn on lights, open the doors wide, heat in the winter, and fans in the summer.

The rabbi saw Cruz's eyebrows form a puzzled furrow and explained. "When our biblical ancestors built the first tabernacle, the Torah tells us it was done with great effort. It was a monumental and holy task but they had to rest on Shabbat just as God had done for the creation. On Shabbat, one does not light a fire. Electricity is a by-product of fire. We light candles the day before Shabbat so that we may bring light into our homes. Cruz recalled his mother lighting candles on Friday, but that was more of a remembrance for Good Friday, so he thought.

"We will respect your faith and family life as I know you will respect ours. You will have much to learn and remember about the Jewish faith and culture. Zachor!—Remember! The Jewish faith is more than a religion, it is a way of life. It is a tradition, it is a culture."

Rabbi Roth continued as Cruz listened intently, catching every word, his blue eyes focused on the rabbi. "You have come to us in our time of need. In two weeks we celebrate Rosh Hashanah, the Jewish New Year. Unlike the secular new year of the Julian calendar, this is the most solemn period of the year and occurs on the first two days of the Hebrew month Tishri. Rosh Hashanah is a renewal of life, a time when we renegotiate our covenant of life with God. Thus begins ten days of penitence. It is a time of prayer and repentance and culminates on Yom Kippur, the Day of Atonement on the 10th day of the month. On Yom Kippur we stand before God as helpless and bare as a newborn, raw with fear and ignorance of our future, similar to a Last Judgment on earth or it becomes annual if we live long enough for another year. On Yom Kippur we confess our sins and reconcile with God."

Cruz listened intently, understanding the English, but those Jewish words were losing him. The Jewish faith had never made sense to him. The only thing he knew for sure is that they had killed Christ and Christ had forgiven them. Today, the mystery would begin to unravel. Unlike his strictly devout wife, Cruz was a relatively nonpracticing Catholic, but he knew about the Last Judgment and confessing sins.

"On the first day of Tishri and the following nine days, a ram's horn, the shofar, will be sounded at sunrise services. It awakens us from our spiritual slumber and urges us to repent. From your home, next to the chapel, you will hear the shofar in the morning as the sun breaks through the desert mountain to the east."

Yes, we would hear it. Cruz's bedroom was on the other side of the chapel, separated by a wall on which a gold-colored framed Nuestra Señora de Guadalupe reigned. Our Lady of Guadalupe, so used to "Las Mañanitas" by mariachis, would now be greeted by the Jewish shofar.

How many times would they wake up to the shofar? For more than forty years Cruz and Guadalupe would awaken to that strange but beautiful ancient musical sound. Each year for nine days, nine times forty, 360 days. The shofar celebrated the creation and God as King of the Universe. In biblical times the ram's horn had been sounded to proclaim a new king. The ram's horn also honored the offering of the ram instead of Isaac as a sacrifice.

The shofar would forever haunt us. As one by one we left home, we took with us memories of awakening to the blowing of the shofar. It was akin to the blowing of a conch by so many other indigenous tribes, but the sound of the ram with a higher pitch seemed more spiritually piercing.

Rabbi Roth continued: "The prayer books in the temple have to be changed. The temple and the chapel have to be ready for the high holidays. Mr. Perlmotter will be guiding you with these details." Mr. Perlmotter had been living in the basement apartment.

Cruz listened intently and, as was his habit, nodded approval with one "hmm" after another. The job had importance, responsibility, and meaning. These were the first of many wise words Rabbi Joseph Roth would impart upon this new employee, a blonde, blue-eyed Mexican Catholic.

The rabbi also hired Cruz to be his gardener. His red brick home with a shady porch and a green garden became an oasis, a cool feast as the jagged desert heat shimmered in the distance.

The Day We Saw God

*D*ios es grande!—Mamá had told us many times but we thought of "grande" as big instead of great. We all knew He was magnanimous but never imagined Him walking past our window one bright morning.

Sure enough, he was big, the tallest person we had ever seen. Our cousin Ninina saw Him first. Her eyes grew, her jaws dropped and she fell to her knees as the gasped, "¡Dios mio! ¡Ahí, va Dios!" We all looked up at the windows and sure enough, it was God Himself in the flesh. Reverently, we fell to our knees and crossed ourselves "en nombre del Padre, del Hijo y del Espíritu Santo." We are awed and overwhelmed by the miraculous apparition though it seemed like a normal appearance. God Himself, white as snow in a brown western suit, cowboy boots, a white shirt, nondescript tie, gold-rimmed spectacles, and curly hair, framing a generous schnozzle.

It made sense. God was at the shul confessing with the rabbi, collecting prayers, His tithes, and checking out the temple. After all, this was the House of God. It never entered our young minds to question if he was the

Catholic god or the Jewish god. Intuitively we knew he was the one and only God.

From the kitchen Mamá heard the commotion and looked into the living room to see us kneeling just as we heard God enter through the front door of the shul, just outside our front door. Before entering, God kissed the mezuzah and then we heard his giant steps going up the stairs to the temple right above us. Our hearts pounded out of our young chests.

Unbelieving, Mamá brought her hands to her eyes, shook her head, and tried to contain her laughter. Jake was an eight-foot-tall giant, son of the reputable Ehrlich family who lived only a block away. Jake was famous and a star in Hollywood where he appeared in movies. He had also traveled with the Ringling Brothers Circus and was also billed as the Tallest Texan, therefore the tallest person in the world. For that, he dressed and acted the complete role with custom-made Tony Lama boots. His car had a sunroof opening for his head and shoulders. Once in a while he would travel back home to visit his family and, inevitably, the synagogue where he had attended Hebrew school and celebrated his bar mitzvah.

Anytime Jake came into town, Cruz was called to the Ehrlich home to set up his custom-made extralong bed. And when Jake discarded some of his clothes, they were given to Cruz and out of one pair of his pants, mother would make pantalones for the kids on her very busy Singer sewing machine.

Once, Efraín and I found an old pair of his Tony Lama boots from a synagogue rummage sale. The boots were so huge that Efraín and I would each get into one of them, up to our waist and then jump around until we fell from the worn heels.

With Jake looking gaunt and too pale for a desert town where the sun spares no one, there was gossip about his failing heart. It was too small, too overworked for such a colossus of a man.

The day he died, the country mourned him, Texas mourned him, the congregation mourned him, his family mourned him. On the day he was laid to rest at Mount Zion Cemetery, Cruz followed tradition and opened the doors to the temple wide open as the cortege slowly drove by. The long specially made casket prevented the rear doors of the hearse from closing and so they tied them together with a rope.

Jake was a kind, gentle, and tall soul with a quick smile who could just as easily have died of a heart that gave too much. He was a god of a man.

Birth of the Temple Gang

*M*y earliest memory of what was to become the Temple Gang brings to my mind the film *The Wild One*. Circa 1946, Efraín, Lupita, and I each had a used tricycle our papá had restored, which we rode around on the outside patio. One day, a group of five rowdy kids, not more than six or seven years old, walked past the patio and looked through the iron gate. Though it was locked, they were small enough to fit through the bars. Yelling and laughing, they chased us inside and took over the tricycles as we watched through a door window. Forty-five years later, the rowdiest of them still stands out. He was Bobby, a natural and unique born leader, with a raucous and soulful laugh, like a madman.

They were going around in fast circles like a circus, laughing and yelling at each other. It was a miniature reenactment of a scene from the *The Wild One*, uncivilized and untamed tricyclists, with Bobby at the helm.

Bobby lived four blocks away. We weren't allowed to cross the street without permission, but here was a kid a quarter of a mile away from home. His father had passed away and his mother worked at La Popular department store. Though he had a babysitter, he was of an independent spirit and kids were mesmerized by his energetic zeal, at times mean, but always with a laugh. Some may have called him a bully, but Bobby also had a heart, intelligence, charm, and a courage that bordered on foolishness and at times beyond foolishness.

Another in the gang was Raymond "El Baby" Telles.

The patio was in the center of the synagogue. Father heard the commotion and came out to chase the kids away. It was our first close brush with urban violence.

Lupita, Efraín, and I were easy targets. We lived in the Jewish Center, were not allowed to cross streets, and we had more of a Mexicano aspect in looks, dress, and talk. Most of the other kids in the neighborhood were at least second-, third-, or fourth-generation Mexican Americans, not all assimilated but pretty well transculturized.

Work and Football

Work at the shul had become tedious and repetitious by the time Efraín and I entered high school. Nonetheless, papá always checked our work. A stickler for details. Papá would give us a severe regañada, scolding, for sloppy work.

"You think I would last long in this job if I did the kind of work you do? You're either going to do it the right way or you aren't going to do it at all!" If he was even more angry, he would dismiss us, "¡Bótense!—Boot yourself out of here! I don't need your help!"

That was the worst, and we would beg to get back on the job. As we grew older we would just walk away. Sometimes angry at ourselves.

We had begun to play school sports, and such time cut into helping papá. He seemed angry or hurt when we were not around to help him, especially during the busiest time of the year, Rosh Hashanah, which was always around football season.

As a farmworker, papá had not only seen us as a family unit but also as a workforce; so from a very young age, we helped him daily after school at the synagogue. Our education was always a priority and if we did poorly in school, he would give us another regañada: "You want to wind up a janitor? Doing this kind of work? That's where you're headed!"

Sports was fun, but somehow, for some reason, it did bother us that papá would have to do all the work we would have done otherwise. Some of the work would be waiting for us or we would do it on Saturdays.

Without knowing the first thing about football, Efraín and I joined the team. I was in the fifth grade. He was in the fourth. Football was legitimized violence, a fun way of almost fighting, wrestling, running, and tackling each other without getting hurt or angry. The pads, especially the shoulder pads, made us look like invincible knights. Nobody wore helmet face masks or mouthguards. Those were only for sissies and kids with braces.

The first meeting after school was to instruct everyone how the game was played. The coach, "Old Man Prieto," explained in his best marine voice all about the T formation and how the number of the play determined who got the ball and which offensive hole it was to go through. Even Manuel, who had just moved from Juárez, repeated the explanation: "Eef da play ees twenty-seex, da number too hofback takes da boll and gos throo da number seex hol."

I was one of the smallest, though I had speed to spare and more moves than "Carter had liver pills." In the playground and in the streets I could literally shift down or up in running speed, make forty-five-degree angles, and literally run circles around those chasing me. This was a great natural gift for self-defense. Most kids found it almost impossible to catch me. Naturally, I was first choice when sides were picked for games like Fox across the River or dodgeball.

After four years of grade school football, I graduated in 1955. Everyone assumed my football days were over, as I weighed only 109 pounds, fully dressed. The year before I had broken my jaw and had my teeth wired together until the break healed. Soon after that I had my appendix removed. I was skin and bones, along with a bad case of acne.

My two buddies, Carlos Lowenberg and Carlos Delgado, tried for the Cathedral High School junior varsity team. Because of their size, position, and experience they had no trouble making the team. My chances, however, were not only doubtful but humorous.

My efforts became a joke. On the way home, two older guys sauntered clumsily along the sidewalk toward me. One whispered to the other, "That's Cathedral's next fullback," and they both laughed. I blushed, flushed with anger, but ignored them.

The first two weeks were calisthenics and grueling spring races. I was one of the two fastest players, though the idea of a skinny little kid beating the best players in sprints angered them.

The third week, football equipment was handed out. The school was so poor that the only pads, helmets, and pants were secondhand discards from the local Texas Western College Miners football team. Most of it had to be repaired. The antique leather helmets had a leather crossband on top that we painted blue and gold just like the Notre Dame University helmets. After a few games the original orange and white Texas Western colors would show through the scratches.

In the dingy football clubhouse, the best equipment was given directly to the first- and second-string players. The rest of us had to take what was left and then exchange among ourselves. In an afternoon of crowded confusion, yelling, and bartering, I was refused any and all equipment. But among the discarded pieces of equipment lying on the floor, I was able to find a pair of cleats that were a couple of sizes too big, some football pants, also a couple of sizes too big, and a practice jersey.

I knew how to remedy the helmet and cleat sizes. The temple had just been carpeted and papá had saved the pieces of leftover carpet sponge. I stuffed the sponge around the helmet for a tighter fit. Later the helmet would swing around my head after I made a tackle. Pieces of foam carpeting also filled the two ends of the pair of cleats. Although the pants were torn and way too big, mamá was a magician with her wonderful Singer sewing machine.

The only item I couldn't find was a pair of shoulder pads. Then I remembered Bavi had an extra pair at home. Fully dressed, I looked like a latter-day Jim Thorpe with pants that ballooned around my thighs. The rest of the team didn't look much better. Dressed in tattered sports clothing that had been discarded, we were now ready for contact.

Naturally, I was again sidelined from all contact except to hold stuffed dummies for the players to hit and the head-on blocking lines. When it came time for scrimmage, I remained on the sidelines.

No matter how hard I tried, making the team became impossible. At the end of the third week, the bulletin board listed the first, second, and third strings. I was not on it. That might have been the end of my football career, but Lowenberg and Delgado urged me to keep going even if I had not made the team.

Coach Bárcena, a former marine, toasted dark brown and with a muscular barrel chest, sized me up and down as if to ask, "Who are you?" but said nothing and then set out to ignore me as he growled to the rest of the team. We never spoke, and I never searched for his eye contact.

Whether it was embarrassing or awkward I don't recall. All I had was the support of two friends and raw determination. Through concentration and prayer I continued to survive on the team. I must have sensed that football was dangerous for someone my size.

Consider some of the head-on exercises. At fifty yards apart, a 180-pound player would catch a punt, and I would run full speed into him in a head-on crash. The only way not to get hurt was to go full speed and not think of the fear, pain, or hurt. At the instant of contact, the churning thigh power of the runner would run a shock through my shoulder and a daze that was almost a welcome relief.

The coach must have begun to take notice but said nothing. I continued with menial tasks, holding dummy canvas bags against blockers.

From the bench I saw us lose the first three games. The fourth game was another boring event against Austin High School. Coach Bárcena walked up and down the sidelines, growling about the end runs against us. With each first down he became angrier at Ramiro, a lanky defensive end.

In desperation he threw his clipboard on the grass and yelled, "Burciaga!" I barely heard my name, then believed he had called it out by mistake or for some menial task. But again he angrily yelled, "Burciaga! Get out there and replace Ramiro!"

I was mentally unprepared and almost shocked. A total fear of failure ran over me. Austin High was having a field day running around Ramiro's side. I ran into the game and received pats of encouragement from my teammates. The cool air was much crisper on the field, and I felt totally exposed to the world. The very next play they came around my end again. I ran into a flock of blockers; two halfbacks, the fullback, and a couple of linemen had pulled out to run interference for the quarterback carrying the ball. Whether it was my size, their disbelief, my speed, or my courage, I don't know. I weaved, hit, and spun around two blockers to tackle the quarterback. I did it two more times until it was fourth down and Austin had to punt. The next time our offense got on the field, Ramiro went in. Coach Bárcena angrily let me know I was permanently on defense. We lost that game and so there was nothing to celebrate, but deep within me I felt a personal victory. I had successfully blocked their end runs.

I have forgotten whom we played next, but the very last game was against Ysleta, district champs every year. I was now playing both defense and offense.

Ysleta had an option play where the quarterback would keep the ball or lateral the ball to another runner if there was danger of his getting tackled. I was fast enough to be inside the backfield before anybody, but the quarterback always lateralled back. Finally I got smart and tackled the quarterback high around his arms, making him fumble as he tried to lateral the ball back.

That was the last of a short six-game schedule. I had been able to play the last three games. Bill Flynn, the Cathedral High School varsity coach, another former marine and Notre Dame football star, was present for that game. He wanted to see whom he was going to inherit for the next season. After seeing us play, he said that I would get a chance despite my size.

We had lost all six games. After the last game, I showered and walked out of the clubhouse, explaining to the coach that I had to return a pair of borrowed shoulder pads to a friend.

A month after the season ended, I would get home, help my papá, and then read the afternoon newspaper before dinner. One day, the sports section carried the names of the All City football team selections for junior varsity. My name jumped out at me. I had made All City defensive end. I read my name again and again until I laid it down to face reality.

I ran outside, down the alley, to the school, the neighborhood, to find friends to tell. I ran exhilarated, unbelieving, filled with happiness. I was lighter than air, my heart beat fast. I had been voted one of the best.

Never again in my life would I ever experience a more meaningful personal victory. No award, mural, book, or other accomplishment would ever compare with the sweetness of that one football season in 1955.

Papá was pleased but never made anything more of it. Despite the loss of his two best and only helpers, he was more pleased that we were enjoying a sport and staying out of trouble. Before television, outdoors was the best pastime, but it also provided the danger of becoming a muchacho vago, a vagabond kid.

From Hebrew School
to St. Patrick's School

*F*irst-grade teacher Sister Mary Lambert was a storyteller of the third dimension as she entranced and enchanted us. From fairy tales to real life drama, from cowboy to Bible stories, each story contained a "moral principle." Principle? I thought that was Sister Noel, the mean-spirited head of the school. What did I know? I was just learning English.

Nonetheless I knew enough English to recognize the story about Abraham from the Hebrew school classrooms, which we helped clean every Saturday morning. Sister Mary Lambert's Bible story is recreated here with artistic license for the sake of levity.

Abraham was a very old and religious man, married to a woman named Sarah. They had been childless for many years until God finally granted them a son named Isaac.

"Abraham! Abraham!" God called.

"Here I am!" Abraham answered. It was in the middle of the night, so Abraham must have been sleeping when he heard God's voice.

"Abraham, I want you to take your only son, Isaac, whom you love so much and go to a land of vision. There on top of a mountain I will point out, you will offer him up in sacrifice."

Now Abraham was a very religious and obedient man. How could he say no to God? He didn't question God as much as he was pained to think that he would have to kill his son whom he loved so much.

In the middle of that night, Abraham got up, saddled a burro, and took with him two young men and his son, Isaac. Then he cut some wood for the sacrifice and set out to the mountain that God had pointed out. They traveled for three days, taking turns riding atop the burro. With each step Abraham carried the pain of having to kill his son whom he loved so dearly. Finally, on the third day, Abraham spotted the mountain.

"You two wait here with the burro while Isaac and I go worship on the mountain." Obviously, Abraham had not told anybody what he was up to. They would have thought him out of his gourd.

Isaac was given the heavy load of wood to cart for his own holocaust, while Abraham carried fire and a sword. Isaac, obedient but no dummy, asked his father, "My father! Behold! Fire and wood? Where is thy victim?"

"God will provide a victim for a holocaust, my son."

"Oh! All right! Behold!" What son would believe that his own father was going to do him in? Isaac fell for it.

They continued together, and when they reached the mountaintop, they both built an altar and laid the wood. When all the work was done, Abraham tied Isaac up and lay him atop the firewood.

No biblical record is available about what kind of resistance Isaac put up, like at least, "Whoa, Dad! What d'ya think you're doing? This is child abuse!"

With his son all laid out like an Aztec sacrifice, Abraham raised his sword and was ready to come down swinging the sharp edge against his son's breastbone and heart. This is the climax of the story. The first-grade class was on the edge of their little wooden benches.

Alas and behold! An angel of the Lord swooped down from the heaven and repeated, "Abraham! Abraham!"

"Here I am!" answered Abraham. Though his real thought could have been, "Where do you think I am, Lord? Hello?"

"Lay not a hand upon the boy or do anything to him. Now I know that you fear God and have not spared your only begotten son for my sake." It was a divine test of faith and obedience.

"Whew!" Abraham calmed down, turned around, and lo and behold! There, stuck in a mesquite brush was a ram. The perfect sacrifice, and Isaac was saved.

I knew the story. Back home in one of the Hebrew classrooms across the hall from our apartment was a calendar reproduction of a dramatic painting showing Abraham atop a mountain, the wind blowing his white beard and robe, the sky purple and orange, his old muscular hand ready to plunge down into his son's young life and an angel swooping down from heaven and grabbing his hand just in the nick of time. How I wished I could show the class the colorful illustration.

Similar to Catholic calendars with colorful illustrations about Christ in the New Testament, the Jewish calendars had just as beautiful colorful illustrations about the Old Testament.

At lunch Lupita and I walked home. Just after lunch, while papá was still sitting down, I excused myself. Quietly picking up my father's keys from the living room I sneaked into the classroom, stood on a chair, and detached the dramatic illustration showing Isaac's near sacrifice. I hid it in a book and carried it off to school.

The classroom was fascinated. Thirty-some boys and girls crowded around my desk to see, gasp, and experience the amazing story of Abraham almost committing sonny-cide. Sister Mary Lambert pinned it up on the bulletin board, and during the rest of the day everyone had a chance to go view it. At the end of the day I pleaded with her that I had to return it to "my friend" who had loaned it to me.

Who was Abraham! El patriarca—the patriarch—the one and only founder of Judaism. Abraham, ancestor to both the Arabs and the Jews. The name Abraham means father of many nations. Interesting . . . Hello, Jerusalem? The Arabs trace their ancestry to Abraham's oldest son, Ishmael, born from Hagar, Sarah's maid, a traditional custom of the times according to the *World Book Encyclopedia*. The Jews consider Abraham their ancestor through poor frightened Isaac.

God also commanded Abraham that all machos in his family had to be circumcised as a symbol of a covenant, an agreement that promised Abraham would have many descendants and Canaan (Israel) would be their everlasting possession.

When his sons were born, papá was given the option of having his three sons circumcised. No way, José. His firstborn was spared the fine machete, and so were Efraín and Raul. Gracias, Papá. Our non-Western tradition continues despite the ridicule we may have gotten in shower rooms.

By the time my sisters entered St. Patrick's, their ears had been pierced, a normal Mexican custom for centuries. The nuns and their Anglo peers thought it barbaric and primitive. And now?

Thus the story of Abraham takes various moral endings, and Sister Mary Lambert inspired me to this day.

Who Killed Jesus Christ?

*C*ruz," Rabbi Roth one day told my father, "the best thing you can give your children is an education." For papá, those words were a jarring reminder of his own lack of formal school learning and the fact that he was married to a former schoolteacher. Mother never once mentioned or thought ill of his lack of schooling, though she constantly and patiently taught him the finer points. Papá had all the social graces and charms, muy campechano—super friendly—but at times he was given to being too frank and too much to the point.

In the Mexican culture there is a difference between being *educado* and being *instruído*. Una persona educada is gracious and ethical. Una persona instruída has had formal instruction. Personas who were both educados and instruídos were admired even more.

So it was off to St. Patrick's Grade School when it was time to attend school. Nine Sisters of Loretto taught the eight grades and kindergarten.

They dressed in long black dresses, and their black hoods in the shape of an M drastically and dangerously reduced their frontal vision in public, in the classroom, and on the playground, and when they drove home they had a ninety-degree windshield view. Just to think of their driving and having to turn all the way at a stop sign or backing out in reverse! They had more than one accident, and in the classroom we literally got away with a few mortal sins and many venial ones.

They became one with the blackboard when writing on it. If they heard commotion from the class, they would have to swirl around 180 degrees like Loretta Young. Their black dresses, bibs, and ample sleeves would continue swirling around their bodies. In the West Texas winds, they were transformed into bats. Their bibs would fly up into their faces.

Our Mexican appearance and lack of English made us perfect targets. We were "You Mexican!" spoken with scorn by our more assimilated Mexican-American classmates, who had learned well in the Anglo-American school system. We considered ourselves Mexican, but in the process of trying to fit in, we did not make distinctions about who they were.

Our friendships and sociability grew, though once in a while they slipped into the mire of insensibilities. It didn't take much for someone to point out that "José is a Mexican, his father is a janitor, and he lives in a Jewish Center."

It was in the dark ages of the forties, when the Baltimore Catechism, the Catholic school system, the Knights of Columbus, the Catholic League of Decency, the Holy Altar Society, and the Catholic Youth Organization all upheld or maintained the assumption, the notion or the idea, that Jesus had been murdered by the Jews. In one way or another, consciously or unconsciously, this was highlighted every year during Holy Week.

We lived only four blocks from school, so we would go home every day for lunch and then run back to the school playground. One day during Holy Week I ran back to a crowd of boys from my second-grade class talking in a corner of the playground. They were talking about me.

"There he is!"

"Yeah, grab him!" Four classmates took my arms, stretched them, and pinned me against the chain-link fence.

The next year another Sister Mary told us how the Jews expected a messiah with the nobility, royalty, and wealth of a king. Neither argument made sense to me, and nobody but nobody questioned a Sister of Loretto's final say and authority on religion. No one!

It was not until October 28, 1965, that Jews were exonerated for any complicity in Christ's death. On that date, 2,221 Catholic bishops from around the world gathered to sign a document entitled *Nostra Aetate*—In Our Time. After fifteen hundred years, the erroneous assumption of Judaism's collective responsibility for Jesus' death was condemned.

Mexico, Loved and Surreal

We lived on the border close enough to the Rio Grande that as kids we hiked across a few rocky desert hills to wade in its cool running waters and fish for tiny minnows. Once a year, during the sweltering summer afternoons, the local paper carried a photo of someone frying eggs on a burning pavement as the chicharras, cicadas, sizzled their song.

To escape that heat, someone would drive us up the Rio Grande into New Mexico and we would float down on black rubber tires. As the Rio entered Texas from New Mexico it would also begin to flow between Texas and Mexico. From this side we would gaze at Mexico's vast powerful desert and raw mountains that daily reflect the pink New Mexico sunsets.

My father had known that desolate desert land across the river as a child. Every time he drove us by the highway along the river he would point it out with an extended arm. "All that land," he would remind us in Spanish, "from that hill there with the adobe ruins all the way to those hills over there, all that land belonged to my father." My grandfather was supposedly a full-blooded Indian who passed away in the great whooping cough epidemic of 1918. "Who knows what tribe he belonged to, but he spoke his Indian language." In those days of the forties and fifties, the hills were empty desolate desert country. Today, the area is populated and has progressed from poor ramshackle colonias without electricity or water to lower-middle-class homes.

He knew the land on this side of the border just as well, for he was born in 1905, when my grandparents migrated back and forth across the border with other campesinos, just at they had done for centuries, following the crops, the seasons, and the reasons. Or as Don Quixote has said many times, "la razón de la sinrazón"—The reason of having no reason.

Like my parents, I had to migrate out of El Chuco to find the cash crops, the seasons, and the reasons after my parents has sowed my future with an education. Over the years since my departure, my physical proximity to that border lessened, but I have returned to Mexico many times since, more intimately and intensely. And here more than ever, I discover the secret this country denies—Mexico never left.

I had not seen my father since 1986, but then in 1991, by the strangest coincidence, I ran into him on a trip to Mexico City, the biggest and largest city in the world, with over twenty million souls. And I came upon him by a one in twenty million chance.

One sunny Saturday morning en la Ciudad de México, before the orange smog stole the blue skies, I took a cab from my hotel to Coyoacán, an ancient Aztec pueblo, now a charming suburbia of Mexico City. The yellow Volkswagen taxicab was brand new, and the driver winced when I slammed the door shut. Because of this, we drove in silence down Avenida Miguel Angel Quevedo and eventually came to a slow stop at an intersection, surrounded by a horde of other smog-spewing vehicles.

I silently looked over to the shady sidewalk. Looking back, I can say it was more of a strong urge, expecting to find something. My eyes climbed up some steps to a high dark volcanic rock wall that resembled a pyramid. Atop sat a man with his back to the street. Instantly, I recognized him. It was my father. His shock of white hair combed back, the peculiar shape of his head, smaller at the top, his ears showing his dark, horn-rimmed eyeglasses barely visible. He wore a blue coat with a western cut. His children and friends always said he bore a striking resemblance to Spencer Tracy, with an Indian nose, steel blue eyes, and the white hair. My father had inherited the blonde traits from our grandmother, a petite, blue-eyed blonde woman of supposed French descent. But Santos Zapata de Burciaga had been as Mexicana as the poorest, with her long dark skirt and a shawl wrapped around her head and shoulders.

I sat in the cab amazed and mesmerized. I had not seen my father in such a long time. The feelings I'd left as a child returned: comfort, strength, a desire to run up to him and in an embrace to kiss him. As a child he would have lifted me up in his strong muscled arms and rough calloused hands. I enjoyed seeing him peacefully resting on the cool black rock. But I was not going to disturb him, for I knew things could never be the same between us.

The traffic light changed to green, and the taxi gently and slowly pulled away. He heard the many cars pulling away behind him, and he slowly turned his head to see. I looked away and immediately hid. I didn't want to see him anymore, and I didn't want him to see me. He had begun to turn his head as if he knew I was there. The taxi went into second gear, third, and we drove away. I hadn't seen my father since he died, September 25, 1986.

The surrealism of Mexico haunts me every time I go back. As a child growing up in El Chuco and crossing to Jarritos every day, I never noticed it. But then I think, maybe this is the surrealistic country and Mexico is the realistic one. Mexico is closer to an ancient culture and the reality of death. All my relatives, dead and alive, are scattered throughout Mexico. While in the United States the culture feigns youth and life.

But in Mexico I recall the wakes of aunts and uncles; caskets occupying the middle of a humble adobe living room or bedroom filled with the smell of burning candle wax. Women wrapped in shawls mumbled Novenas, Letanias, Ave Marías, and Padre Nuestros, while in the next room compadres drank mescal and in hushed voices traded gossip about the deceased.

One of the last times I saw my father was in an El Chuco hospital. He had already suffered a stroke and could not communicate. The hospital overlooked the edge of the vast Mexican desert from the Rio Grande that glistened like a silver ribbon in the landscape. He had resigned himself to his furious struggle against old age and infirmity. His one reminder to us always, forever growing up, was, "No te hagas viejo"—Don't grow old. And now he had resigned himself to the inevitable. He no longer had to be strapped to the hospital bed.

That late afternoon, my Irish-American cuñado, Clete, and I took him outside from his hospital room in a wheelchair. My cuñado offered my nonsmoking father a cigarette. My father smiled. He could no longer laugh. We passed a gobernadora tree. Clete cut a leafy branch that gave the desert its smell and placed it in my father's hand. He gently held it, looked at the branch, and raised it up to smell the desert. His eyes looked up to where the sun had just set and then turned to his left to the rocky dark brown of his other country, a land he had known so well. His eyes became intense and then relaxed to the memories of a much earlier time. He couldn't speak, his

The End/El Fin. This is the end, ¿Qué no?

lips were pursed, but his eyes said it all, traveling through his youth. ¡No te hagas viejo! The Mexican revolution, riding the rails, dances, compadres, his father, and his vida as a father. He had seen his tierra and he was at peace. The sol had set over the New Mexico horizon. It would soon get dark, so we took him back. That was the last time I saw him, I think.

About the Editors

MIMI REISEL GLADSTEIN is the author of four books and coeditor of one. Her scholarly articles, covering subjects as diverse as the Harry Potter series and bilingual wordplay in Hemingway and Steinbeck, have been translated and published in both Mexico and Japan. Gladstein has been recognized internationally with the John J. and Angeline R. Pruis Award for teaching Steinbeck and the Burkhardt Award for Steinbeck scholarship. She is currently president of the John Steinbeck Society of America. At the University of Texas at El Paso she has served as associate dean of liberal arts, chair of the English department, chair of Theatre, Dance, and Film, and was first director of the Women's Studies Program. In 2006 she received the University Distinguished Achievement Award for Service to Students.

DANIEL CHACÓN has two books, *and the shadows took him* (2004) and *Chicano Chicanery* (2000). He has completed his second novel, *Black Sound*, and is working on a collection of stories, *Unending Rooms*, and a memoir tentatively titled *At Play in the Quantum Field*. His fiction and essays have been anthologized in such books as *Humor Me* (University of Iowa Press), *The Best Latin-American Erotic Fiction* (Penguin), *Our Working Lives* (Bottom Dog Press), and *Floating Borderlands: Twenty-five Years of Hispanic Literature* (University of Washington Press). He has stories and essays in such journals as the *New England Review, Colorado Review, ZYZZYVA,* and *Callaloo*. He is currently a professor of creative writing in the bilingual MFA program at the University of Texas at El Paso.